William Robertson, W. F Robertson

Our American Tour

Being a Run of ten thousand Miles from the Atlantic to the Golden Gate

William Robertson, W. F Robertson

Our American Tour
Being a Run of ten thousand Miles from the Atlantic to the Golden Gate

ISBN/EAN: 9783337188856

Printed in Europe, USA, Canada, Australia, Japan

Cover: Foto ©Andreas Hilbeck / pixelio.de

More available books at **www.hansebooks.com**

BEING

A RUN OF TEN THOUSAND MILES

FROM

THE ATLANTIC TO THE GOLDEN GATE,

IN THE AUTUMN OF 1869.

BY

WILLIAM ROBERTSON AND W. F. ROBERTSON.

VIRTUTIS GLORIA MERCES.

Edinburgh:
PRINTED FOR PRIVATE CIRCULATION
BY W. BURNESS, PRINTER TO HER MAJESTY.

1871.

DEDICATED

TO

MY REVERED AND VENERABLE

FATHER.

W. B.

CONTENTS.

CHAPTER		PAGE
I.	THE VOYAGE OUT,	1
II.	HOTEL LIFE,	5
III.	ON THE HUDSON,	11
IV.	SARATOGA,	14
V.	THE SHAKERS,	18
VI.	AMERICAN MILITARY MEN: BARBERS,	30
VII.	ALBANY, VIA LAKE CHAMPLAIN, TO MONTREAL,	33
VIII.	MONTREAL,	37
IX.	A NIGHT ON THE ST. LAWRENCE,	39
X.	QUEBEC,	42
XI.	OTTAWA AND THE RAPIDS,	45
XII.	NIAGARA FALLS,	50
XIII.	CHICAGO,	53
XIV.	AMERICAN CHURCHES,	60
XV.	OMAHA: AN UPSET,	63

Contents.

Chapter		Page
XVI.	ACROSS THE PRAIRIES TO CALIFORNIA, .	67
XVII.	SALT LAKE CITY: MORMONISM,	71
XVIII.	ON THE PRAIRIES AGAIN,	79
XIX.	SAN FRANCISCO,	84
XX.	ST. LOUIS,	95
XXI.	LOUISVILLE AND THE MAMMOTH CAVES,	100
XXII.	WASHINGTON: CHURCHES, WHITE AND BLACK,	108
XXIII.	WASHINGTON, .	111
XXIV.	RICHMOND, . .	114
XXV.	NORFOLK: FORTRESS MONROE: PHILADELPHIA,	118
XXVI.	A NIGHT ON THE SOUND: BOSTON,	124
XXVII.	NEW YORK, . ..	129
XXVIII.	CONCLUSION, .	139
APPENDIX,	.	145

PREFACE.

The following pages are the substance of familiar wayside jottings sent home to fireside friends during a hasty tour in the United States of America and Canada, accomplished in the brief space of eighty days, travelling at the daily rate of some hundred and forty miles.

In such a rapid run over a country of such vast dimentions—from Canada to California—only the surface of the country, and of the people and their ways, could possibly be seen or described. What we saw and heard in this cursory way, and the first impressions made thereby, are here reproduced, in response to many assurances that the story of our adventures would possess a personal interest in friendly eyes, and yield, to those within our circle, a portion of the pleasure we have experienced in thus preserving the recollections of what was to us a rare, an instructive, and a happy holiday.

Tay Park, 1871.

CHAPTER I.

The Voyage Out.

ON the 10th of July 1869, we waved adieu to our friends from the deck of the noble steamer "Cuba," and, under happy auspices, steamed down the Mersey. The saloons, the state-rooms, the whole appointments, and in particular the weather, were great improvements upon those described by Charles Dickens in his account of his trip to Boston, on the occasion of his first visit to America, in the good ship "Britannia." Assured that the Cunard line had never lost the life of a passenger, and surveying our magnificent vessel, with her excellent arrangements, her able captain, picked officers and men, we felt satisfied that neither the lifeboats nor lifebelts, so plentifully provided, were likely to be required. A quiet order prevailed on board, every officer and man was at his post, doing his appointed duty with a military precision, which to us was reassuring as well as novel.

A sea voyage must always be less or more monotonous. The chief incidents are breakfast, luncheon, dinner, tea, supper; relieved by the games of shuffle-board, deck quoits, cards; reading also for the retiring, flirting for the gay, betting for the bagmen. In the evening, concerts from the sailors on deck, Scotch songs from the passengers in the saloon; high jinks too, by the crew, who, dressed up as donkeys, bears,

West-End swells, fine ladies, and so forth, paraded the deck, sang songs, and enacted their rude farces. The hat went round, and the Yankee passengers, ever profuse, showered down a silver rain in return to "Jack" for his amusing performances. More profitable it is to recall the pleasant Sabbath we spent at sea, the tolling of the bell for service in the saloon, the passengers assembling, the tars in their clean Sunday rig taking their places, and the singing of the psalm to an old Scotch tune, led by the manly voice of our gallant captain. Most becoming and impressive it was thus—our ship a speck on the mighty deep—to call upon Him

> "Who plants His footsteps in the sea,
> And rides upon the storm."

To minister well at sea, the parson sometimes requires to be a good sailor. The Atlantic rollers will not be charmed to stillness even by the best of sermons. One good clergyman, whose head was sounder than his stomach, had to beat a hasty retreat one Sunday, after having just managed to delay the catastrophe long enough to bring the sermon to a decent conclusion. He did not reappear for several days.

A whale or shoal of porpoises in sight, a passing ship, sunset and sunrise: these are all interesting events at sea. At half-past three one morning, we got up to witness sunrise at sea—to us an unusual sight. The sea was calm as a lake; even the great rolling swell of the Atlantic was almost entirely at rest. At four, exactly, the watch was changed. To the minute the relieving officers appeared, the bearings of the ship were exchanged, and having refreshed the inner man with a cup of coffee and a sandwich, brought by the night steward from below, the new officers scrutinized the appearance of things in general, and then assumed their measured tread at stern, amidships, and at bow. Precisely at 4·30 the first glimpse of glorious day appeared. Gradually the horizon became gilt with golden tints, which quickly spread and rose higher and higher, till in two minutes' time, the whole circle of the sun was visible, and a flood of burning golden light set all the eastern sky aglow. It was a truly grand and memorable scene.

> "With flames of piercing light
> He bursts in glowing majesty !
> Hail, O glorious sun !
> Thou source of light and life, all hail !
> Hail, O glorious sun !
> Sublime and universal orb,
> O earth's pervading soul,
> Creation cries all hail ! "

At five o'clock next morning, the eleventh day from Liverpool, we were awakened by the boom of cannon, the signal for the medical inspector. We were off Staten Island. At length the doctor's tender came alongside, and having received a satisfactory report of the company's health, we slowly steamed to Jersey city. Alongside the quay at last, our patience was yet further tried, for Her Majesty's mails must first be landed, and eager friends on shore must postpone "the kissing" till the bags are off. At length we are upon American soil, and in the hands of the Philistines, who first appear in the shape of custom-house officers of the baser sort. Schedules must be filled up, locks opened, trunks unpacked. The uninitiated do not know that in this free country the golden key is the great "open sesame." At last a big chalk mark is upon each "piece" of our goods and chattles, and we are turned out upon the quay into a quagmire of rotten planks and mud, and to the tender mercies of New York hackmen, perhaps the biggest scamps that ever whipped a nag, or went unwhipped themselves.

Our first impressions are not reassured by the wretchedly paved streets and tumble-down wooden buildings through which we pass, till the precincts of the landings both at Jersey City and New York are left behind. The huge ferry-boats, like floating railway stations, strike the new comer, and Noah and his ark naturally occurs to one's mind. These ferry-boats ply betwixt Jersey City and New York, and also betwixt Brooklyn and New York, every two or three minutes, all day long. Each boat accommodates about twenty carriages, which are driven right on board, with their "fares" inside, and in addition some hundreds of foot-passengers in separate saloons, the whole being comfortably under cover.

CHAPTER II.

Hotel Life.

AFTER a drive of some two miles, we reached Fifth Avenue Hotel, at the head of Broadway. It is a splendid white marble edifice, capable of accommodating about eleven hundred visitors, and is usually crowded. . We were fortunate enough to secure apartments. The charge at this hotel, as at most of the first-class American hotels, is five dollars per day, and this includes board, lodging, and attendance. The ground-floor of the building is occupied by the office, the billiard-room, the "bar"—a handsome white marble counter, where gin-slings, brandy-smashes, whisky-cocktails, sherry-cobblers, lemonades, and the other numerous and mysterious liquors of Yankeedom, are concocted and vended—a railway ticket office, telegraph office, post office, carriage office, cigar-shop (segar, the Americans spell it), news-stand, reading-room, barber's shop,—the whole being floored with marble. The large entrance hall, also on the ground-floor, generally contains piles of baggage of arriving and departing guests, sufficient to load many railway waggons; and in the evening it is thronged by several hundred persons, who here meet to smoke, talk, liquor, and expectorate.

Having entered our names in the guests' book, which is invariably the first preliminary on arriving at an American hotel, our bed-room key is handed to one of the numerous porters always in waiting. "Biddy," the chamber-maid, receives us graciously, assuring us she is from Ould Scotland too. (In America it is common for the Irish to represent themselves as Scotch.) Wherever we went we had reason to be proud of our country. To be a Scotchman is to belong to a country of honest, able, and religious people, whose sons and daughters, for the most part, do honour to their country. Such is the reputation Scotland enjoys, not only in America, but all over the world. Long may she sustain her great repute! Fifth Avenue Hotel is the crack hotel of America. The grand staircase is of white marble; the dining-room is floored with white and brown marble, diamond pattern, and can dine three hundred persons at one time, the company being seated at numerous tables capable of accommodating ten or twelve each. The apartment is an oblong oval, lofty and elegant, the decorations being in white and gold. Seventeen windows, reaching from floor to ceiling, and an equal number of handsome mirrors of the same dimensions, give it a noble appearance. The stairs, breakfast-room, luncheon-room, drawing-rooms, corridors, and vestibules, are covered with rich and beautiful velvet carpets, which yield luxuriously to the foot. Their delicacy does not save them from a liberal baptism of tobacco juice from both guests and servants, who prefer the carpets to the spittoons upon which to discharge, being in this, as in everything else, wholly "regardless of expense." A vertical railway plies almost uninterruptedly from basement to upper floor, in which guests are conveyed, in an elegant apartment, up and down, to and from their rooms.

The servants, both male and female, in this hotel are almost all Irish. The waiters are less smartly dressed than in the old country, and are much less obsequious in their services. They do obey orders, but it is with an air which says, "Remember, one man is as good as another here, if not a good deal better." "Bring me a glass of beer," said I to our waiter. He replied gruffly, "Are you going to pay for it?" "Of course I am." "Give me money, then, and I'll fetch it," was the rather rude reply. The common drink at table in American hotels is iced water. "We live on ice," said an American lady It is not the custom to drink beer or spirits in the dining-room, but only at the bar, which is usually a separate concern and under different management, though an adjunct to the hotel. Wine is very dear and very bad, and by Americans scarcely ever drunk:—"The truth is," they told us, "we don't know good wine from bad."

American cookery is an imitation, but nothing more, of that of France. Daily an elaborate programme is printed and laid before you at breakfast, dinner, and tea; that for dinner containing from thirty to forty different dishes, besides a dozen different vegetables, and as many relishes. It looks very grand—on paper; but somehow it was unsatisfactory, to us at least, in practice. Breakfast, luncheon, dinner, tea, supper, goes on pretty much from five or six A.M. till eleven or twelve P.M., and any one having a fancy that way may occupy his whole time in the different saloons where these recreations are going on. A Yankee, in ordering dinner, tells the waiter to bring pretty nearly the whole programme. Having selected what suits him, the balance left over may be reheated for the next comer. However this may be, the meats had a "cauld kail het again" flavour about them that was not at all agreeable to our tastes.

Fifth Avenue Hotel was one of the most comfortable that we visited, and is ably managed. We have also pleasant recollections of the Riviere House, Boston; Willard's, Washington; Cataract House, Niagara Falls; Galt House, Louisville; the International at Norfolk; the Continental, Philadelphia; and the Occidental, at San Fransisco. All these establishments are comfortable and excellently conducted; all upon a large scale, and some are models of elegance and convenience. The Galt House, Louisville, was newly opened when we visited it, and was the most perfectly arranged hotel that we met with. The building covers a block or square measuring about two hundred and forty feet on all sides, and of some six storeys in height. The court in the centre of the square is occupied by the grand entrance and dining-hall. The grand entrance-hall is about forty-five feet wide, and two hundred feet long, floored—as is usual in American hotels—with marble in chequers, and is adorned by handsome pillars. In and adjoining the hall are the office of the hotel, railway ticket and telegraph offices, cloak-room, baggage-room, smoking-room, reading-room, writing-room, &c. An elegant elevator raises you in a twinkling to any floor. The stairs are six feet wide, and so easy, that a horse might be ridden up. There is a suite of three drawing-rooms, two of which measure about forty-five feet by thirty, and are furnished with exquisite taste and elegance. The carpets of the whole house are of the richest description and most beautiful designs. The bedrooms are large and airy. Ours measured about twenty-eight feet by seventeen, and was free from bugs and mosquitoes—a rare luxury in America. The corridor of the drawing-room floors is about forty-five feet wide, the ceiling supported by pillars. On this floor is the ladies' private boudoirs, ladies' writing-room, and ladies' hairdressing rooms. On each bedroom floor there is a porter's office, with which electric bells communicate, and there an attendant is always in waiting. In this hotel there are about six hundred apartments, all newly and most elegantly furnished, airy, and comfortable.

In America the hotels are a great institution, in extent and splendour far exceeding anything with which we are accustomed in this country. While they are used by the crowds of American travellers, who are ever on the move, they are also largely supported by families who make them their permanent home. In a country where the young ladies marry at fourteen and sixteen, and the gentlemen at sixteen and eighteen, the hotels become the homes of such precocious couples. The gentleman is not in a position to furnish a house, and the lady votes housekeeping slavery and a bore. Families of pale-faced puny children are reared in these gigantic establishments, where notices may regularly be seen warning them not to make a playground of the corridors. Having no natural liberty, the poor things must be ladies and gentlemen from their infancy; and it is questionable whether they are not born with their hair neatly parted and lilliputian rings upon their tiny fingers, prim and trig, just as they appear at the public tables, at ages when our old-world notions would have them romping in the nursery or on the green.

The result of this hotel life is bad. It is bad for the young couple, and very bad for the children. Where five hundred to a thousand people are housed together, the chances are that all will not be saints; and in America morality is not better, if not worse, than in the old country. What the consequences are where so many young and inexperienced girls are exposed to temptation without occupation or household duties, is too well known in American society. Eating, gossiping, dressing, and reading trashy novels are preferred to the cares of the household and the nursery. Babies are too often voted a bore, and one of the social problems of American life is the fewness of American born children, the encouragements of baby shows notwithstanding. In these hotel establishments the quiet and social enjoyments of our family circles are unknown,—the vital influence of parental example and precept upon the young scarcely felt. Brought from their infancy into the whirl and excitement of these promiscuous crowds, hearing the smart sayings and glib oaths of their seniors around, the young too soon copy what they hear and see. Their infant lips utter smart sayings, and baby oaths are too often encouraged by those around, if not, alas, even by their own parents, whose counsel and restraint they quickly learn wholly to despise. It is not uncommon to see children of ten calling for liquor at the bar, or puffing a cigar in the streets. In the cars we met a youth of respectable and gentlemanly exterior who thought no shame to say that he learned to smoke at eight, got first "tight" at twelve, and by fourteen had run the whole course of debauchery. Hotel life and want of proper early home training appear to be working the moral ruin of vast numbers, while the extravagant style of these palatial establishments accustoms the young couples to habits of lavish expenditure, which follow them into their maturer years. "Enough for the day is the evil thereof," appears to be the maxim of the fast American. "Eat, drink, and be merry, for to-morrow we die"—or, as he would probably render it, "Let's liquor, for to-morrow we burst!"

CHAPTER III.

On the Hudson.

AT eight o'clock A.M. we got on board the steamer "Daniel Drew" for a sail up the Hudson to Albany. The morning was lovely. The steamer, 950 tons burden, dashed along at the rate of about eighteen miles an hour. Being the first American river boat we had been on board of, we noted with special interest her build and fitting up. She was altogether unlike anything we had ever before seen afloat. On the lower storey or floor was the dining-room, on the second floor the drawing-room, and a series of private sitting parlours at either side, from the windows of which family parties were enjoying the splendid scenery in all the comfort of privacy. The furniture and carpets of these rooms, public and private, are of the handsomest description,—sofas, couches, easy chairs, in blue silk velvet and tapestry work. The staircases and other woodwork is of polished walnut, bright and shining. The promenade on the third deck is delightful, as the steamer shoots smoothly over the placid waters of the Hudson. The scenery on either hand is very fine, not unlike that of the Rhine, and though less picturesque, is yet highly interesting. We pass West Point, the site of the American Military School; Newburg, where the American army was disbanded after the War of Independence; the Katskill Mountains in the distance, and other points of interest. At the widest point the river extends to about four miles across, and varies to about half a mile at other points. The water, like that of most American rivers, is muddy. It contains large numbers of lanky sturgeon. We passed many sloops and lumber boats, one tug steamer dragging twenty-eight of these behind her.

Our steamer had on board crowds of Americans out for the day,—husbands and wives, children and maids, sweethearts and lovers,—all dressed in holiday attire, gay and glittering. We could not but remark, however, the difference in style as compared with our home ladies and gentlemen, and the comparison was not, I fear, complimentary to our American cousins. The stranger does not at first take kindly to the rough and ready manners of our go-a-head friends over the way. Your seat is appropriated without a "By your leave." You are rudely jostled without a "Beg your pardon." It is every man for himself, and no compromise. "Self" appears in all his naked ugliness, with little care to round off the sharpest angularities.

This was the first time we came into contact with Negro servants, and the impression was not favourable. We acquainted the black steward that we wished to dine at three, and punctual to the minute appeared at table. To our chagrin, the grinning black informed us that dinner was over, and the greasy tablecloth betokened what we had to expect. Wretched, ill-cooked, out-of-season scraps were all we could obtain. On complaining to the master of the cermonies that we had fared so ill, all the comfort that we got was an indifferent "Ay, have you though?" but no apology or explanation.

Nevertheless we had a capital day of it, and arrived at Albany at half-past five in the afternoon, where we took up our quarters at the Delavan House Hotel. I have good cause to remember this hotel, for it was here that I was first introduced to that interesting acquaintance, Lady Mosquito. For a fortnight after, the swollen and inflamed arms of one of our party kept him in happy remembrance of Albany. If he goes back he will not forget the lesson as to the treatment of mosquito bites; for of all the many cures, "Let them alone" appears to be the best. At all events, whatever you do, don't rub them, and don't scratch them, for the wicked brutes themselves could not wish you worse than that.

CHAPTER IV.

Saratoga.

ALBANY, so named after James II., contains about one hundred thousand inhabitants, but possesses little of interest; the chief building being the handsome Roman Catholic Cathedral, which can seat about four thousand persons. The streets are ill paved, the houses mostly of brick, and of an unpretending character. From this city we made an excursion to the celebrated Saratoga Springs thirty-two miles per rail from Albany. This was our first experience of American railway travelling. We were tickled by the novelty of the cars. Having secured our tickets at the office—a wretched wooden shed—we proceeded to take our seats. We found the train promiscuously at the side of the street, all innocent of covering overhead, or even fence of any kind. The ordinary American car is about sixty feet in length by about ten in breadth. It is seated for about fifty passengers. The seats hold each two persons, and are ranged on either side of the car with a passage between. The seats are handsomely cushioned with plush, and there is a good-sized window for each. The doors, two in number for the whole car, are situated at either end. Conveniences, such as in the old country are found at the stations, are fitted up in the American car, one at each end. The indelicacy in a

European's eyes of these arrangements, does not appear to strike American ladies and gentlemen. Certainly, in some respects, this system is the best. Iced water is supplied in summer gratis in the cars, usually from reservoirs in either end, but if not so, by a servant from a pitcher. This is a great luxury and comfort, in fact an indispensable necessity in these long, hot, and dusty journeys. The wheels of the cars are of cast iron, and smaller in diameter than with us, while the springs are inferior, and therefore the riding is rougher. The track is usually only a single line, and the road more roughly made than in Europe. Wood being plentiful, the sleepers are laid close together, which admits of the rails being used of a lighter section.

On our road to Saratoga we passed through a country under cultivation, but not so fully farmed as at home; stumps of the old forest trees being still left in many of the fields. The farm-houses were made of wood, and of a poor character. We saw scarcely any live stock. Saratoga's chief attraction is the wonderful mineral springs which abound there. The most popular are the Congress, the Empire, the Columbian, the High Rock, the Iodine, the Pavilion, &c. A new one had been discovered shortly before our visit, the most pungent of them all, so bitter that a mere tasting satisfied us.

We drove round and visited the most noted of the springs, partaking of the waters, the various chemical properties of which are chloride of sodium, with proportions of carbonate of soda, carbonate of lime, carbonate of magnesia, carbonate of iron, sulphate of soda, potassium, carbonic acid, &c. Previous to the discovery of these springs by the Americans, one of them at least was known and used by the Indians. The High Rock spring is the most interesting, owing to the curious rock formation from which it issues. This singular rock is of a conical shape, and is formed by the accumulated deposit of the mineral substances held in solution by the carbonic acid gas contained in the spring, viz., magnesia, lime, iron, &c. It rises to about three and a half feet from the surface of the ground, and in the ground is a circular hole, say of one foot in diameter, from which the water issues in a bubbling effervescing state. Less or more, this is the condition of all the springs, some boiling like an angry pot. Congress waters are bottled and sent all over the world.

In the vicinity of Saratoga there is a curious Indian village or encampment, consisting of a street of some two score wooden huts or booths, in which the creatures dwell in primitive simplicity, subsisting upon the proceeds of their bead work, baskets, cushions, and chip curiosities, bows and arrows and such like, which they expose for sale from the little stalls in front of their dwellings. They generally speak English quite well, and are tolerably civilized in their habits, clothing, and appearance. Some seemed to be pure Indians, and others of mixed extraction. The scenery of Saratoga is not remarkable, and excepting the singular mineral springs, there is nothing to attract. The inhabitants, in winter, number only eight thousand or thereby; but in the season visitors arrive in crowds from all parts of the Continent, as many as a thousand a day sometimes, so that the population in summer swells to about thirty thousand. The town is chiefly built of wood, and the business is lodgings. There are several hotels, but the great resort is the Congress Hotel, just completed, and probably the largest establishment of the kind in the world. The dining-room is capable of seating comfortably fourteen hundred persons at one time. The drawing-room measures about seventy feet by forty-four, carpeted and furnished in the usual magnificent style. After our drive we halted here to dine, and were shown quite unceremoniously through the drawing-room, then occupied by elegantly attired ladies, into the dining-room. In America every door is open, and free to all comers, whether prince or peasant.

Saratoga being in its glory when we were there, the ladies

were very gay, in white, and silks of blue, rose, pink, lavender, and all the hues. They chatted at the open windows, cooling themselves with their fans, and listening to the band of music maintained by the proprietors of the establishment, or promenaded upon the piazza in front. Dinner at this hotel cost us a dollar and a half each, equal to 4s. 6d. sterling. The waiters were all blacks, of various shades of blackness, to the number of about fifty, and when not on active duty, were stationed like rows of ebony pillars on either side of the dining-hall, forming a striking contrast to the white-painted walls. They were civil and obliging, but slow. One smart French waiter would probably do the work of three Negro waiters, and do it far better.

CHAPTER V.

The Shakers.

IN America the spirit of freedom appears in every custom and habit of the people, and in every institution of the country, but in nothing more strikingly than in the religious sects, with doctrines strange and wild. It is the land of Mormons, Tunkers or "Harmless People," Bible People or "Perfectionists," Spiritualists, and Shakers. Strange it is that the most extraordinary developments of most of these creeds is connected with the propagation of the race. The Mormons are to renovate the world by a multitude of wives, and a rapid multiplication of descendants; the Perfectionists are to perfect society by living together like a herd of cattle, annulling all laws of relationship, both human and divine; while the poor Shaker is to cleanse the world, and end it at the same time, by ceasing to propagate the species altogether.

In the neighbourhood of Albany is one of the settlements— that formed by Mother Ann Lee, the first prophetess of the order —of these latter comparatively harmless religionists. It was on one of the few uncomfortably warm days (heat 82° Fahr. in house, and 105° in sun at mid-day) which we experienced during our sojourn in America, that we drove out a distance of some six miles to attend the Sunday services at the Shaker village of Watervliet. The way lies by a plank road, the first that we had met with. It is constructed simply by levelling down the worst inequalities, and laying longitudinally close together rough wooden planks. In a new country, well supplied with timber, a tolerable road is thus speedily made at little cost. A toll of five cents each way was charged. The Shaker village is situated in a well cultivated district of country, broken in by the diligent hands of these industrious creatures. They live in "families," the men and women separate. They do not marry, and have no children. Their ranks are recruited from without by such as care to follow their strange ascetic life: chiefly by orphan children, the poor, the helpless, and the fanatic. The village consists of the church, a plain brick building; the Shaker store, the sign over which is simply "The Office," and some six or eight large wooden dwelling-houses where the "families" reside. Their occupation is farming, and they are famed for their seeds, preserved fruit, brushes, and such like; Shaker goods being at a premium in the market, and known to be of the best and most honest of their kind. They are a sober, hard-working, quiet, and thrifty people, reputed to be in comfortable worldly circumstances, and of austere and upright life.

Following the example of the Jews, the Shakers separate the sexes during public worship. Over the twin doors of the humble tabernacle, we found painted up on the left, "Males," and on the right, "Females." Our party separated accordingly, not without a "shaky" feeling at the strange arrangement. Having taken our seats amongst our fellow males, we had time ere the service (or performance) began to survey the curious place. Four-fifths of the house was reserved for the brethren and sisters, and was entirely devoid of pews or seats of any kind, excepting a few forms ranged round the walls in dancing-school array. The Gentiles were accommodated in two little galleries at the one end, infant school fashion, railed off from the rest of the house, the ladies in one, the gentlemen in the other. The day was fine, and the curious from all parts assembled, some on foot, others by conveyances, which were ranged, unyoked, along the village road. A veritable male Shaker sat inside the railing which divided the meeting-house, as the Gentiles took their places in the galleries appointed for their accommodation. A mild and gentle little man he was. The cut of his hair and of his dress were, to say the least, slightly peculiar, and evidently not of the latest Paris fashion. The hair was straight as straight could be, cropped short in front, but long behind. The breeches were of brown, the vest of blue, of the long capacious mould of ancient days; coat he had none, but his snowy shirt sleeves were tied in by a riband above the elbow. This curiosity sat motionless, a study in creation, while the common male and female herd took their respective places in the galleries. Ever and anon the good man rose and counselled the audience in gentle tones to make room, reminding them of the sin of selfishly appropriating more than necessary space, when it might be their brethren and sisters would have to stand throughout the service. His appeals were respectfully attended to, and when no more could be packed outside the railings, he opened the little gate, and admitted the audience to the sacred precincts.

At length the time arrived, and with much interest we watched what followed. On either hand, at the opposite end of the meeting-house, were two doors, which by-and-by opening we could perceive two strange and motley crowds, the one of males, the other of females, ridding themselves of shoes and hats, and assuming their dancing slippers. When properly attired they entered in two streams, each sex apart, and with a mincing tiptoe step in single file proceeded to their seats on either side of the church, along the wall, the floor all clear, as for a dance. The sisters seated themselves round on the one side, and the brethren on the other. The sisters were dressed much alike, in light-coloured cotton dresses, *sans* crinoline, white napkins on their shoulders, and on their heads starched caps or " mutches " of the sow-back breed. The brethren were dressed similarly to the one already described, and both males and females carried over their arm a mysterious little white towel, which on sitting down they placed upon their laps, emblematical no doubt of their virgin purity. Both males and females were, with few exceptions, hideously ugly. Seated in silence, their hands demurely folded over their towels, they presented a strange and even weird appearance, suggestive of a lunatic asylum out for a holiday. Their numbers were about one hundred, half being males and half females; while in age they varied from boys and girls of ten or twelve, to old men and women of seventy and upwards. One fat Negress was amongst the sisters. At length by one consent they all got up, and approached each other face to face in lines upon the floor. A brother then commenced the proceedings by remarking, confidentially, that this was a beautiful morning, for which they should feel duly thankful; and not only for that, but for all their other blessings,—for health, for the comforts of life, and for the peace which reigned amongst them. That the peace and comfort which they enjoyed was an evidence that they had indeed chosen the true road to happiness. That by denying themselves not only sinful pleasures, but those which were in themselves not sinful, and by living a spiritual and celibate life, holding communion with the spirit world and with each other, not as mortals, but as regenerate spirits, heaven would to them be begun on earth; peace, love, and joy would be theirs in an angelic sense, even now here below. After this short address he said "Let's sing," and forthwith they bellowed out with might and main, in marching time, what, being repeated again and again, sounded to our ears to be as follows:—

"From the dark shades of earth
   I'll away, I'll away,
 To my home in the better land;
 There the trumpet is sounding,
 And I hear the angels say,
 There is rest, there is rest
   In the better land."

After they had repeated the above many times over they stopped, making a kind of bow or salaam towards each other. Then another brother made a little address, very much in the same terms as the first, inculcating self-denial, goodness, and chastity, and especially extolling the virtues of the latter, arguing that thus living heaven was to them begun on earth, and that hereafter in the invisible they would enjoy perfected blessedness. Then "Let's sing again," he said; and off they went for another few minutes with the remainder of their hymn:—

> "Toil on, struggle on,
> There is rest, there is rest;
> If the cross you can bear,
> The crown you shall wear;
> For there is rest, there is rest
> In the better land."

At this point a Methodist minister of Washington entered, and was accommodated with a seat inside the railing. He was afterwards recognised and welcomed by the Shaker pastor. A friend of this Methodist minister informed me that he occasionally visited the Shakers; not that he agreed with them, but that in his opinion every one should have religious liberty. What say our strait-laced sectarians to such an all embracing liberty as this?

The Shakers having rested a little, again got up, this time ranging themselves so that the sisters had their backs to the audience, and the brethren facing their partners as for a dance. The hymn was again struck up to a jigging tune, and they all commenced to trot backwards and forwards, singing as they shuffled and turned, and turned and shuffled, meanwhile flapping their hands and arms in a most singular manner. The whole thing was so intensely grotesque, the old creatures singing, trotting, and flapping, that it was with the utmost difficulty we retained our gravity. Having thus shaken themselves to their hearts' content, and warmed their old frozen limbs, they all retired to their seats, the virgin napkins were again laid upon their laps, male and female, and their hands were folded in angelic style. A young Shaker of thirty-five years of age or so, then stood out upon the middle of the cleared floor, whether to dance a minuet or to preach a sermon we did not know, but it proved the latter.

He began by stating that he had been disappointed of some one to address us (which, by the way, we found was a stereotyped apology in similar assemblies in America), but that he could not do better than enlighten the Gentiles outside of the railing as to the history and principles of their society, regarding which there prevailed great ignorance and misconception. It was alleged, he said, on the one hand, that they worshipped an old woman, and on the other, that they lived together in discord and hatred, the men hating the women and the women the men. Neither of these notions was correct; for they loved their sisters, and their sisters loved them with a love pure and heavenly, far exceeding the gross loves of earth. True, the old Adam might sometimes rise within them, and an unloving word might be spoken; but then the spirit of Christ was absent, and when it returned, confession and reconciliation took place. Then they did not worship an old woman. Mother Ann Lee, as they loved to call her, was the founder of their order; but they did not worship her, but only the spirit of Christ manifested in her. He did not wish to say anything that would shock the ears of those who differed from them, but he frankly told them that, inasmuch as they did not worship Mother Ann Lee, neither did they worship Jesus. But the spirit of Christ was in Jesus, and it was also in Mother Ann Lee, and they worshipped Christ in both. Jesus was their spiritual father in Christ, and Mother Ann Lee was their spiritual mother in Christ. They could not be spiritually regenerated without both a father and a mother, and there could not be a father without a mother. Ann Lee was the mother, and she was specially useful to the sisters, understanding all their peculiar troubles and temptations, and standing by them, even as Jesus was a spiritual father to the brethren, specially sustaining and comforting them. To Christ they look for regeneration, and He was developed corporeally first in the man Jesus, and secondly in the woman Ann Lee. Jesus was a mere man, even as Ann was a mere woman. Both might have broken the laws of man many times, but neither ever broke the laws of Christ; both kept His laws perfectly. He had no doubt that Jesus had broken the Jewish laws legions of times, just as Mother Lee had broken the laws of Great Britain and America. Jesus became a great teacher only after He was baptized by the Spirit; and Ann was baptized by the Spirit in the same manner, before she also became a great teacher. Their great call in life was to know the spirit of Mother Lee, the consort of Jesus, and His equal in purity; for the spirit of Christ was equally developed in both. Jesus they take as their Saviour, to lift them out of the abyss of sin and degradation; but there is a necessity for a spiritual mother, in whom to be conceived if they are to be born again, therefore they prize Father Jesus and Mother Lee alike.

Mother Ann Lee was born, he told us, in Manchester on 29th February 1726, of poor parents; so poor that they were unable to give her any education, and therefore she was never taught to read or write, and could do neither. She was a quiet and sedate child, and did not mingle with other children in their games and play. She grew up as other children do, and wrought at the cotton factories. She had feelings and affections like other young women, and she was courted and married. She had several "small" children, who, however, all died in infancy. After the death of her children, Ann became still more sedate and retired in her manner, and became very unhappy and dissatisfied with her condition and way of life. Finally she had dreams and angelic visits, from which she learned that her true road to happiness was to leave her husband and live a virgin life. These spiritual visitations had a great effect upon her, so much so, that when under them she actually trembled and shook in a most marvellous manner.

At that time there was in Manchester a split from the Quaker body, of those who were more zealous, called the "Come-outers." Amongst this earnest sect Ann met with kindred spirits who sympathised with her, and ministered to her religious consolation. Her spiritual gyrations increased; she became gifted with tongues, and ultimately was chosen the leader of the "Come-outers." In their public worship, the Spirit descended upon them with such power that they were shaken in their bodies, and even cast down upon the floor. This was the reason that ever after they have gone by the name of "Shakers," or Shaking Quakers. Such was the intolerance at that time in England, that the police apprehended Mother Lee on a charge, forsooth, of dancing on Sunday, and cast her into prison. There she was confined fourteen days and nights without food, but Joseph Whittaker, her adopted son, fed her through a chink in the door with wine and milk, which he introduced by a straw! Upon her release from prison, it was remarked that notwithstanding this scanty diet, she was in better corporeal condition than when she went in. The persecution to which she was subjected did not prevent her from continuing to celebrate religious worship according as she was moved by the Spirit. The numbers that were attracted to her meetings increased, the shaking dance was joined in still more vigorously, not according to the present order, but entirely according to the movements of the Spirit. Again she was apprehended for Sabbath desecration, and this time brought before ten judges, who demanded that she should give an account of herself. She replied that she was entirely unlearned, could neither read nor write, and could only answer if the Spirit gave her utterance. The judges pressed her, and thereupon the Spirit came upon her, enabling her, to the astonishment of the court, to speak in no less than *fifty-two* different languages! This so confounded the bench, that they let her go unharmed.

Ultimately Mother Lee received a revelation directing her to flee from her persecutors to a spot on American soil: upon that exact spot he, the speaker, then stood. Eight Shakers in all, five males and three females, one of the men being possessed of some worldly wealth, accordingly took their passage by the "Maria" from Liverpool. Upon the passage the ship sprang a leak, and, strange as it might seem, this proved a fortunate circumstance for Ann's reputation as a prophetess. During the voyage the Shakers had regularly practised the religious dance on Sundays, but the captain, a rough man of the world, made light of their zeal, and threatened to cast them overboard if they did not desist from what he superstitiously considered Sabbath desecration. Now that the ship was in a sinking condition, he blamed them as the cause of the disaster, but no threats would induce Ann to stop the dance. She, however, declared to the captain that an angel, at that moment standing by the mast, had revealed to her that not a hair of the heads of any of them should be harmed. At that moment a great wave rolled against the ship, and the leaking plank started back into its place. Ann rose in the captain's estimation immediately; they stopped pumping, and, resuming their dancing unmolested, they pursued their voyage without further mishap. In due time, upon the 16th day of August 1774, they arrived at the spot upon which they were now settled. The place was then an unpromising and dismal swamp, the site of the church in which they were then assembled being a pool, into which they cast trunks of trees to form a foundation, but here Mother Ann was directed to abide: "Here," she said, "shall I build my church."

For some three years they laboured in their forest home, clearing the woods, tilling the land, turning the wilderness into a garden. But the War of Independence came, bringing trouble with it to the settlers. They refused to fight, being men of peace, protesting against all war. Their neighbours, suspecting them for spies, took them before a magistrate, requiring them to take an oath of allegiance to the Republic. But their principles allowed them neither to swear nor fight. Ann and her flock were cast into Poughkeepsie gaol. Here again she spoke with tongues, communing with the spirit world. When released from prison, Ann's fame as a prophetess had spread far and wide. Having, amidst these trials, fulfilled her times, and a time and half a time, Mother Lee was perfected —that is, in the language of the world, having lived three years and a half in America, she died, or rather disappeared from view, for with Shakers there is no such thing as death in the ordinary sense of the term; they only disappear bodily, but their spirits hover around and commune, as when in life, with their mortal brethren and sisters. Before disappearing, she appointed Joseph Meechum as her visible successor.

Ann, though so highly gifted, was of singular humility, refusing the worship offered to her by the brethren and sisters, saying she was but a woman. She did the lowliest work, washed the feet of the community, ate the crumbs from the common table. They desired to be like their dear Mother Ann, as they loved to call her, to follow in her footsteps, even though she was an old woman as the world called her; not because she was a woman, but because the spirit of Christ was in her. She lived a virgin life, and only thus restraining the natural affections could the world be regenerated from the fall of Adam. The Gentiles did not believe that they lived as they said they did, yet their then society had existed generation after generation without one single case of impropriety having been brought against them. It was only because those outside the railing doubted their own ability to live a chaste, self-denying life that they suspected them. Nevertheless, true it was that all of them, brothers and sisters, were pure as the napkins on their laps. Miss Stone and others agitated for the elevation of women, their right to the ballot, and so forth, but such would never give them true elevation. True elevation, true peace, true happiness, would only be found in the community of the Shakers, where all things were in common as in the Pentecostal days of old. Neither Mother Lee nor they, male nor female, exercised their right to vote, nor did they seek the protection of any law against each other; they were governed solely by the laws of equality and love, pure and heavenly, far stronger, far dearer than earthly love, and to this true enjoyment, true happiness, and true repose they invited the poor, the weary, and the downcast.

Such was the Shaker sermon or address, almost in the exact words of the speaker. The Gentile audience were then informed that they might change their position if agreeable, by standing a little, of which permission advantage was thankfully taken, as we had of course remained sitting throughout, joining in no part of the Shaker worship, which, indeed, had altogether taken us by surprise. We were quite unaware of the absurdity, not to say profanity, of the whole performance. The Shakers now formed themselves into two circles on the middle of the floor, the women forming one circle, the men surrounding them in another circle, the leaders of the singing, or rather bawling, in the centre of all. The tune, after the style of "John Brown's body lies mould'ring in the dust," being struck up, they flippered round and round, singing, shuffling, and flapping their hands, first palms upward, then palms downward, and round about by jing-go-ring; then reverse and round about by jing-go-ring again. Old decrepit, hobbling male creatures, dressed in fantastic antediluvian fashion, short-cropped hair in front, long elfin locks behind, slippers on feet, little towels over their arms, there they skipped and clapped, hobbled and jumped, shuffled and skipped. Boys and youths, got up in the same ridiculous style, imitated as well as their inexperience could the so-called shakings of the the spirit. The female creatures were no less active, the older and uglier the more they shook, the younger women following suit. Only one or two goodlooking ones could we observe; one rather pretty Shakeress had a touch of sly sadness under her close clapping mutch. But the song they uttered this time sent a cold thrill to our very hearts: it was a hymn of praise to Mother Ann Lee. The only part of the words we could make sure of were—

> "To whom do I owe my gratitude?
> To my mother, my mother.
> Her goodness and love how can I repay?
> My mother, my mother!"

We were getting by this time impatient to be away from the scene; indeed, one of our party had already made for the door. But the whole was drawing to a close. After the last blasphemous chant, they had salaamed and taken their seats once more. One of the oldest females here got up, and feebly echoed the concluding sentiments of the preacher. She had been a happy Shaker for some thirty years, living a life of virgin purity and celestial love—serenely happy—heaven begun below—no strife—no contention,—peace, quiet abiding joy. The outside world might not believe these things now, but the time would come when they would see that the Shakers were the only true people, the regenerators of the world. The finishing hymn was then sung, somewhat to this effect:—

> "We live to God, the greatest and best,
> We live to God, the greatest and best;
> Give me bread that is pure, and water that is clear,
> Give me bread that is pure, and water that is clear."

They once more salaamed in their own peculiar fashion, then hobbled to their seats. The Shaker usher then thanked the Gentiles for their quietness and attention during the service, and told them they were "dismissed;" and so the service ended. The number of spectators present might have been one hundred and fifty, and no unseemly remark or noise was made during the strange proceedings. Such is the wretched, silly, and blasphemous system which in free and intelligent America has found thousands of adherents. The seven that pinned their faith to Ann's skirts, and sailed with her in the "Maria," have grown to eighteen separate societies, all more or less prosperous. Every great religious excitement or revival, it is said, adds to the number of these deluded, demented creatures.

CHAPTER VI.

American Military Men—Barbers.

THE Barber's Shop is a great institution in America. There the barbers are artists and gentlemen. Their stylish establishments are specimens of elegance. They pay handsome rents, and charge handsome fees. Our barber's shop at Delaven House Hotel, Albany, was no exception. The rent equalled £350 a year. In these establishments you may be shaved by a major, or shampooed by a general. My artist at Albany was only an ex-lieutenant. Had seen, according to his own account while officiating upon my headpiece, twenty-eight engagements, but had never been hit. Did not believe the bullet could be cast to hit him; none of his family had ever been hit. Enjoyed the war with the South, and would like another, not particular with whom. England he would like to have a shy at, and believed they would lick her. Made a good deal of money in last war, but spent it; would like to make some more, and would take better care of it. Americans the finest soldiers in the world; would take any quantity of fire, but would not yield, by —— ! When in the South, entered the planters' houses, did as he pleased, and helped himself; came out swell on Sundays with the jewellery he stole in the war. The planters a set of bad fellows, lived with black women, and then, when tired of them, sold both them and their children, and did this again and again. Knew such cases himself. These stories may be taken for what they are worth. This youth informed me he could return to the American army at any time, resuming his rank as lieutenant. Whether truthful or not, he was a smart fellow, and could both crop and talk smartly, differing wholly in manners from the same class of artists in this country; considerably in advance too in his charge for his services, which was half-a-crown.

This fast youth, and other two young New Yorkers, were the only parties that expressed to us any feelings of hostility to Britain. The sense and substance of America is for peace, only the froth and scum for war. The Americans, like ourselves, have too much to do in minding their own business, to want anything but peace. They want to trade, to make railroads, bridge rivers, cultivate their millions of acres, develop their iron, coal, and cotton, extinguish the Mormons, settle the Indian territory, and pay their debt; when these things are done, they will be ready to fight if occasion arises, or even before then if need be, but war will not be of their seeking. The "Alabama" claims is only a party cry, and political capital for Mr. Seward and others, but the nation says, " Let them go; we may yet pay Britain back in her own coin when the time comes,"—the time of her necessity. The military of America are her artisans, clerks, shopkeepers, merchants, lawyers, doctors—gallant, daring, dashing men, ready to work, or ready to fight. When the war fever raged, it was hard to keep these mettled fellows from the field. Even young Scotchmen, not ten years out of Dundee, as in one sad case in Philadelphia, would not be kept from the war, and though wounded and invalided once, yet were not to be restrained from again rushing to the fight. Sad, sad to think that friends never knew whether their lost ones fell fighting on the field, or died of starvation in the wretched prisons of Andersonville; and such was the spirit, such the fate of thousands.

It is astonishing with what rapidity an American changes his profession, and how readily he adapts himself to any new set of circumstances. One general, whom we met, was a farmer and manufacturer of agricultural implements; another gallant officer was a merchant in Boston; another, a general, a merchant in Philadelphia; another, a major, an insurance agent in Richmond. Those who, like Grant and Lee, had the advantage of being educated at West Point Military School, of course, came to the surface before those who learned military phraseology, as many did, on their first march. Grant is universally considered an honest man, with firmness and determination, but not genius; his success, it has been remarked, was insured by drowning out the war with the dead bodies of his troops. Lee is on all hands admitted to be the greater man, though on the losing side. Teaching a military school at Lexington for his daily bread, and refusing a proffered public testimonial from the ruined South, he presents a spectacle of dignified adversity, which excites the deepest regard in the South, and even the respect of the victorious North. It is to be regretted that his estate near Washington is so utterly destroyed, by being made the location of liberated slaves, and the burying-place of those who fell, that it is unfit for being returned to him, even if the repeal of the Act of Confiscation could be obtained.

Since this was written, I regret to add that Lee died at Lexington, where he was head of the Military College. He was not only beloved by the gentlemen of the South, but men of the North knew and revered his intellectual capacities and his true nobility of character.

CHAPTER VII.

Albany, via Lake Champlain, to Montreal.

ON leaving Albany we took the cars to Whitehall, on Lake Champlain, proceeding thence by steamer on the lake to Plattsburg, where we again resumed the cars for Montreal. This was our first experience of railway travelling in the United States. At the ticket-offices—which are not only situated at the stations as with us, but are also usually scattered throughout the cities in the shops and at the hotels—there is only one class of ticket sold. Formerly, indeed, there was only one class of carriage to be had, but now there are practically three classes; the drawing-room car answering to our first-class; the ordinary car, into which only ladies, or gentlemen accompanied with ladies, are admitted; and the smoking car, into which all gentlemen, unaccompanied with ladies, whether smokers or not, are incontinently consigned. The two latter are one price, but for the drawing-room car an extra charge of one dollar per day, or for any portion of a day, is charged. This extra charge is collected by the conductor after you have been seated. Upon this occasion we took our seats in the drawing-room car, into which we were shown by a Negro. We found it extremely elegant, airy, and comfortable. The car or carriage measured about fifty feet long and ten feet wide. As usual there were only two doors, one at either end of the car. The interior was divided into three compartments, consisting of two private parlours, each affording accommodation for eight persons, besides a saloon containing twelve easy chairs and two sofas. The easy chairs were fitted upon swivels, enabling the luxurious occupants to turn in any direction at will. Both saloon and private parlours were handsomely carpeted, as well as otherwise fitted up with every regard to taste and elegance. From the large windows on either side, the country could be conveniently viewed; while by them, the ventilators in the lofty ceiling, and the doors, abundant ventilation was obtained. In special charge of the car we had a conductor, who favoured us with his company on the next easy chair: our black friend, his assistant, also pays us a friendly visit now and again; while Luke the labourer, Jack and Jill from up the hill, stroll through at their own sweet will for change of air from the smoking car. Such things strike a stranger at first more than they do after a while. We could not help picturing to ourselves the horror of the Honourable Lady Selina Silk Stockings, or the Most Noble the Master of Touch-Me-Not at home, if the guard, the coal-heaver, and the navvy from the third class should hobnob with them in the first class in this free and easy style. I am bound to say, however, that all our visitors were gentlemanly and polite, bearing themselves quite as if used to drawing-room company—more mannerly by far than the same class at home; the natural result, no doubt, of the mixing of class with class, which both levels up and levels down—so that in America, all being upon an equality, you miss the wide diversity of manner and style which so separates the high, the middle, and the lower classes at home.

But suddenly our musings are stopped, and so is the train, right in the fields, far from any habitation. There was only one line of rails, and no telegraph available, so that a collision, or at least a long delay, appeared inevitable, for on getting out to see what was up, we found that the drawbar having snapped, the engine had taken leave of the train, and bidden us good-bye. Moreover, there were no coupling chains, but merely the two-inch iron drawbar, while even this had been partly worn through before starting. It was quite amusing to see with what *sang froid* the Yankee travellers, conductors, and engine-drivers took the whole matter, not even removing the cigars from their mouths. " Fix him with a chain!" cries one; but lo and behold no chain was to be found. " Hand me the poker," cries another, and " I'll fix him for you right away!" The poker was accordingly handed over, and the big Yankee proceeded to form a hook upon each end of it, whereby to attach the recreant engine. With a plentiful contribution of oaths, the stoker at length fished a piece of chain from beneath his coals, wherewith at last we got "fixed," and so proceeded, once more, on our way rejoicing.

This was on the 26th of July, the day beautifully bright, and along the line the reapers were harvesting wheat, hay, &c. The fields were still partly uncleared of the blackened stumps of the original forests, and the farming on the whole seemed quite inferior to what we see in Scotland. Leaving the cars at Whitehall, we embarked on board of the charming little steamer on Lake Champlain. Here we had the pleasure of enjoying an excellent dinner, clean, well-cooked, and smartly served. Thanks to the deference paid to our lady travelling companion, we had the privilege of the first admission to the dinner table. One penalty that bachelors and those having no lady friends have to pay in America, is to wait till their betters are served. Gents, when you go to America, be sure to take your wife, sister, or cousin with you, or look out for the toughest steak, the coldest soup, the worst seat in the cars, the hardest bed, and the highest attic!

The sail up Lake Champlain was delightful, the scenery pleasing, but not equal to that of our own Loch Lomond and Loch Katrine. Still the Andirondack Mountains, thickly wooded, rising behind us in ever-varying light and shade, the rocky margin of the lake clad with pines, clutching the riven fissures with their roots, and then the perpendicular rocky cliffs above, presented a very interesting scene. (As we sailed along we passed two iron smelting furnaces on the side of the lake.) At Burlington, the capital of the State of Vermont, the lake widens out, so that the shore becomes almost invisible from the steamer. The cars were waiting for us at Plattsburg, which is nothing more than a landing-place on the lake. The country through which we pass here is not particularly interesting, but being new to us, we enjoyed it. The land is only partially cleared of the pine forests, but here and there are little farms, with small wooden dwelling-houses, with now and then pleasing hamlets growing up around the various railway stations. The soil appeared to be stony and light, the crops by no means satisfactory; still the children scampering around had freedom and fresh air, and we could not help contrasting their happy faces with the squalor of our lanes and closes at home.

From Plattsburg to Montreal is a distance of about eighty miles. When nearly half-way we entered the Canadian territory, where we were visited by Her Majesty's officers of excise, who inquired respectfully as to the contents of our hand-baggage. Complimenting us upon our "honest" appearance, they accepted our word of honour that we had nothing worse than a flask of cognac, and passed us without examination. It was night when we reached the River St. Lawrence. Our train was noiselessly put bodily on board the ferry-boat, and in a few minutes we were landed on the Island of Montreal. Another half-hour brought us to the city. After getting our baggage passed by the custom-house officers, we got into a carriage, and reached the St. Lawrence Hall Hotel at eleven o'clock P.M., quite ready for bed.

CHAPTER VIII.

Montreal.

MONTREAL, the principal city in British North America, contains about 150,000 inhabitants. The island upon which it is situated is formed by the Rivers Ottawa and St. Lawrence. The quays, streets, and public buildings are substantial, and even handsome. The site upon which the city is built belongs chiefly to the Roman Catholics, and the finest building in it is the Cathedral of Nôtre Dame, which is said to be capable of seating ten thousand persons, the same number that is accommodated in the Mormon Tabernacle of Salt Lake City, these two being the largest places of worship on the American continent. There are five other Roman Catholic churches, besides many Episcopal, Presbyterian, and other Protestant churches. There are also three Roman Catholic nunneries.

The situation of Montreal is very fine, being upon rising ground at the base of Mont Royal. In the suburbs are numerous beautiful residences, occupied by the merchants of the city. A striking feature of this city is the glittering tin-covered roofs of the houses, tinned iron plates being the universal substitute for slates. The two greatest public works are the Water-Works and the Victoria Bridge. The supply of water is obtained from the St. Lawrence at some distance above the city, where there is a fall sufficient to give the motive power which pumps the water up to the reservoir from which the city is supplied by gravitation. The Victoria Bridge spans the St. Lawrence at the city, connecting it with the opposite shore. It was constructed by the Grand Trunk Railway Company, and is only available for their railway. It is 9194 feet or nearly two miles in length, and consists of a heavy iron tube resting upon twenty-four piers, and two abutments of masonry. The central span is 330 feet in length, under which the steamers plying upon the river pass and repass freely. This magnificent bridge, which was inaugurated by the Prince of Wales in 1860, cost upwards of a million and a quarter sterling. It has been called the eighth wonder of the world, but I hope ere long we shall have a ninth and greater wonder in the Tay Bridge at Dundee. At the Montreal end of the Victoria Bridge there is an enclosure containing the bodies of six thousand immigrants, who died of ship fever in 1847, over whose remains the workmen employed in the erection of the bridge have erected a monument to commemorate their sad fate.

Montreal is a busy, thriving, commercial city, and was rendered all the more interesting to us, in that we there met with several old Dundee friends, with whom we spent some pleasant hours, communicating the news of the old country, and receiving information of the new. Last summer the heat here was excessive, and deaths by sunstroke common. When we were there in July, the thermometer stood at 78° Fahrenheit in the shade, but we were not incommoded by the heat.

CHAPTER IX.

A Night on the St. Lawrence.

AT 6.30 P.M. we embarked on board of the steamer "Montreal," of the French Company's line, for Quebec; ticket, 12s. each; distance, 180 miles. With your ticket you receive a key for your bed-room, which is clean, neat, roomy, comfortable, each usually containing two berths, married persons' berths being different from those for single parties. On board there is accommodation for three hundred passengers. The steamer is a three decker; saloon about 220 feet long, about 13 feet wide, floor to ceiling about 18 feet in height. It is lighted by handsome chandeliers suspended from the ceiling. The carpets, sofas, chairs, settees, are handsome, elegant, and luxurious. A piano is there for the amusement of the ladies. Gay crowds promenade around, chatting, smoking, reading, card-playing. A party of soldiers are on board bound for home, going to join a British man-of-war awaiting them at Quebec. Of course they have a "wee drap in their e'e," and keep the steerage in a stir. They sing and they bawl. The strains of "Annie Laurie" in the distance, remind us of "Maxwellton's Braes," and of "Bonnie Dundee." Wherever we have gone, though Scotland is left far behind, not so her songs, which are as common here as at home. The evening is most beautiful, the waters of the mighty St. Lawrence, here two to three miles wide, roll down in calm majesty, floating us on their bosom at the rate of eighteen miles an hour. The sun sets gloriously, and night then quickly closes around us as we retire to rest in our floating palace home.

At half-past five next morning we arrived at Quebec. The gong rouses us, and taking our traps in our hand—dressing first of course—we step on board of another smaller and very much inferior steamer "the Magnet," here in waiting, in which we pursue our course to Ha-Ha Bay, on the River Saguenay, 335 miles from Quebec; fare £2 : 2 : 6, returning included. This trip was recommended to us by our Montreal friends, but we did not find it sufficiently interesting to repay the time it occupied—fifty-nine hours. At the mouth of the river there is a small village and a large hotel, where the *élite* of Montreal and Quebec come to spend their summer holidays, but we saw nothing of interest in the place at all. It is famous for mosquitoes, if that can be called a recommendation. Americans told us that even residents who have been in the country for many years, are subject to be bitten if they pass from one state to another. The mosquito appears to know at once whether you belong to their country or not, for *natives* in the same boat with us were not bitten, while our party were all but torn to pieces by the brutes.

During the night we passed up the river to its head, viz., Ha-Ha Bay. Around the bay there is a small village, but from the poor nature of the ground, the people must have a very hard time of it. The soil appeared to be nothing but stones and brushwood, and how the inhabitants manage to subsist we cannot tell. There is a small lake a few miles farther up the river, where the Hudson's Bay Company have a station for buying furs, &c. from the Indians and hunters. The River Saguenay is 1800 feet deep at some parts, the water being of a brown coffee colour, and from the mouth to the source it is hemmed in by lofty hills, covered with low stunted pines, which give the colour to the river. This river is proverbial for the immense quantity of fish it contains, which are so numerous that they are said to be "anxious to be caught:" however, the quality of the fish over all the continent, so far as our experience went, was not equal to our own Tay or Tweed salmon, or fish of the German Ocean.

The interesting points of this wonderful river are about half-way up, and concentrate at Trinity Bay. Here there are two gigantic rocks, with strange and dismal names; one is called Cape Trinity, 1500 feet, and the other Cape Eternity, 1800 feet in height. They overhang at the top just as if a shake would send their heads thundering to the bottom. In the bay there was a death-like silence, which, combined with the dark pine woods surrounding, produced a very solemn impression. It must be very miserable living here in winter, when the river is frozen, precluding all communication with the outer world. What inducement the French could have had to people such an uninhabitable portion of the earth is known best to themselves. Probably they may have been ignorant of the grand country to the west. The summer here lasts only from three to four months, and the winter from seven to eight.

We were delayed at Tadousac by the fog, which prevented us from continuing our voyage up the St. Lawrence as soon as we wished. When waiting in the steamer, we were visited by a party of Indians, who had come across the St. Lawrence from Riviere de Loup in a small bark canoe. There were four of them, one man and three women. They had come across to sell little baskets, ear-rings, and model canoes made of bark and wicker-work. One of the women could speak French very well, but the others could talk only the Indian language. We bought a small canoe, very neatly made indeed. We saw them paddle away after they had done trading, and the young lady paddled in the bow of the canoe just as expertly as she had done the trading with the strangers.

CHAPTER X.

Quebec.

THE best hotel is the St. Louis, where we stopped. Quebec is an old French town, and everything in it partakes of the French character. The people talk French, the streets have French names, and the town is built in the old French style. We went and inspected the Citadel, which covers with its many buildings the summit of Cape Diamond to the extent of about forty acres. We got a most splendid view from the ramparts, both up and down the St. Lawrence, as well as of the other side, where there are several more forts being erected for the better defence of the river. The condition in which we found the Citadel was not what should have been expected, from the position that Quebec holds. The accommodation for the men who had their quarters under the ramparts was worse than that provided for our criminals at home. We visited the Plains of Abraham, one and a half miles beyond the St. Louis gate. The place where Wolf landed his troops is a very high bank, and very steep, requiring great valour on the part of the assailants. We also inspected the field where Wolf had his decisive encounter with Montcalm, and the spot where he breathed his last, which is covered with a neat monument, bearing the following inscription:—

"HERE DIED WOLF VICTORIOUS,
13TH SEPTEMBER 1759."

Even the Houses of Parliament are not free from the general decay and dilapidation which is so visible in this comparatively ancient town. The houses contain two neat chambers, the upper and lower, two reading-rooms, and a library. The fibre matting on the lobbies and the paper on the walls were full of holes, and discoloured. We took a stroll through the narrow, dirty, ill-kept timber-paved streets to the Bank of Quebec, to cash one of our Coutts and Company's circular notes (which, by the way, we found, whether in Europe or America, the most convenient and best known kind of documents). We here got some more information as to the current money in the dominion, the variety of which to foreigners is a constant source of trouble and vexation. The foundation of their currency is the cent = our halfpenny; 100 cents = one Canadian dollar, 4s. 2d. sterling; four dollars eighty cents = £1. But gold being at a premium, we got 20s. 3d. per pound: silver, on the other hand, being at a discount, we are obliged to submit to a deduction of about four per cent. when paying any considerable sum away. When trading, however, shopkeepers never ask the discount, their prices being fixed according to the rate thereof. English shillings pass here the same as quarter dollars, and there is no discount on "bankable funds," that is, the paper money of the established Canadian banks, gold, Bank of England notes, Coutts and Company's circular notes, &c.: on these there is generally a premium of 3d. per pound. In many of the shop windows "silver for sale" may be read; in these shops "greenbacks" may also be bought and sold, but there is no certainty of the price, as money changes value every day. The fact of so many different kinds of money passing current is to a stranger very confusing, and the confusion is increased until you discover that it is the custom here to call their own Canadian twenty cent silver pieces by the name of shillings, and their ten cent pieces sixpences. For instance, say you go and change a sovereign, they will tell you that you have got 24s. 3d. for your pound, and you will begin to rejoice that you have found a country where the Queen's image is so highly valued; but on examining your change you will find that it is Canadian currency you have got, which not being "bankable funds," are subject to a discount of four per cent. if you offer them to hotel-keepers, bankers, or money-changers. Formerly this delightful state of hodgepodge was further confounded by "York" shillings, worth sixpence, and ever so many more different kinds of money.

We left Quebec for Sherbrooke, glad to escape from the heat, dust, and discomfort of the city. Sherbrooke is half-way to Montreal, and on our way we passed through 101 miles of forest, where a few settlers were trying to make a living by tilling the poor pine-clad and rocky soil. Sherbrooke contains about four thousand people, and is rather falling off than increasing; but it is beautifully situated, and has great water power from a river running through the town, which is utilized for a paper mill, where paper is produced from the linden tree, &c. We stayed over the Sunday with a kind and hospitable clerical friend, and next day continued our way to Montreal by the Grand Trunk Railway; but the name belies it, for the road is very rough, and the plant very bad. In length it is 1400 miles, but that is the only grand thing about it. The land, after we had passed St. Hyacinth, becomes much better. On the outskirts of Montreal we passed through good clay soil, covered with crops of barley, wheat, Indian corn, potatoes, &c., in fields of American dimensions,—probably a mile long by a quarter of a mile broad. This was the first really good land we had as yet seen in the States or Canada.

CHAPTER XI.

Ottawa and the Rapids.

WE left Montreal by the Ottawa River, and sailed up to the city of Ottawa, the new capital of the dominion. We enjoyed the scenery extremely. On the way up we passed a large number of rafts with as many as from thirty to forty men upon some of them. These rafts are taken down as far as Quebec, and there broken up and sold. The people live on them all the way down the river, and they resemble floating villages. They build little wooden houses, just like dog couches, upon the rafts, and indeed men and dogs live together. The city of Ottawa is most beautifully situated, being right upon the edge of two perpendicular rocks, over which the river rushes. From the deck of the steamer it had a very fine effect. The sun shining upon the water made it glisten, while all around there were hundreds of rafts teeming with human life. It is here that the new Houses of Parliament of the dominion have been built, and very fine structures they are. They are above the city, and have a most imposing appearance, being similar in style, and, at a distance, look not unlike Westminster in miniature, or say in cabinet size. We drove over the suspension bridge and viewed the magnificent scene presented by the Ottawa Rapids, which are terrifically grand.

The rugged rocks and the angry hissing waters, boiling and surging down at the rate of, I should say, twenty miles an hour, present a scene never to be forgotten for its picturesque grandeur. Nor is the interest lessened by the fact that to this stream is largely owing the prosperity of this fine and thriving city.

On the banks of the river there are a large number of saw-mills, all driven by this mighty force. These mills go night and day, just like our own iron-works at home, and employ large numbers of men, cutting and arranging hundreds and thousands of logs of timber. The same watery agency is utilized to bring the timber right up to the edge of the saws. We also saw the process of shooting uncut logs of timber down to the river below. Men seated themselves on the end of the trees, and at certain intervals sluices were opened, and away they went at such a breakneck pace that one would think men and timber would both be found dashed in pieces at the bottom.

We left Ottawa very well pleased with our visit to it. To all appearance it is the most thriving city in Canada; and as it is well situated, it ought to become at no very distant period one of the first cities of the dominion.

In doing the St. Lawrence, one always shoots the Rapids. This is a very interesting and exciting kind of enjoyment. It consists in rushing down the Rapids at the speed of about twenty or thirty miles an hour. The long Soult Rapid is the first and longest, the Lachine is the fourth, last, and most dangerous. It is very exciting being shot down the boiling waves amidst rocks and shoals on all hands, feeling the steamer apparently sinking beneath your feet as she shoots down hill, the white-crested waves dancing and leaping around; but there is really little or no danger, for the pilots—some of them Indians—are trained from their boyhood in the management of rafts and steamers as they shoot these Rapids. We passed, on our way down, a steamer which had sunk on a rock a short time before. No lives were lost, except one soldier, who had foolishly leaped, in his consternation, into the river, and of course was drowned. At one part of the Rapids we passed as close as within from six to seven feet of one of the numerous rocks, the tide rushing like a mill-lade, but only a few ladies made any noise; they gave one or two slight screams, but as for the captain, he only took his pipe out of his mouth for a few minutes at the most critical point.

After passing the Rapids we went under the Victoria Bridge. A most splendid structure it appeared from the river below. From the rapidity of the flow of the St. Lawrence, the enormous descents of ice in winter, and the other engineering difficulties, the construction of this bridge proves that the proposed Tay Bridge at Dundee presents no insurmountable difficulty. The Montreal Bridge, which is nearly as wide as that proposed to be erected over the Tay, was constructed at a great distance from the base of operations, and when experience in such structures was much less mature than now.

When we reached Montreal we again departed at once for Prescott on our way up the St. Lawrence through the justly celebrated Thousand Isles. This part of the river, and the scenery along with it, is one of the most beautiful points on the whole continent, and is only surpassed in beauty and magnificence by the Falls of Niagara, and by the Nevada Mountains, away far west. The river at this point is about four miles wide, and is thickly studded with small rocky islands, covered with trees and brushwood. On one of these some one has erected a small house, which, with the romantic nature of the situation, adds to the picturesque effect. The only thing that is wanted is a nobler background. If the mountains of Switzerland were here, the effect would be surpassingly grand.

We stopped two hours at Kingston for the purpose of taking on board firewood for the engines, and had time to take a walk through this thriving place. The town is well built and pretty clean; all the streets are, as usual, at right angles, and are lined with trees to give a cool shade to foot-passengers. There are also some very good public buildings of stone, and the town is well defended by martello towers and forts.

We met on board this steamer an old Dundee mill-boy, now a large wood-merchant in Florida. He had all his property destroyed in the war betwixt North and South, in which also his brother was killed. He himself had served in one of the Southern regiments. This gentleman was of opinion that the South will do better now than ever they did with slavery; but he lamented that in the meantime the liberated slaves, by their votes, have the Government of the country too much in their own hands, and that it is being very badly and corruptly managed. The liberated slaves, he said, are working well, and he was employing and paying some of his own former slaves himself. This man is an example of how one may thrive and prosper in a new country if he will only apply himself. A lazy man is of no use in such a country as this; here, if a man works, it is rarely that he will not succeed. All the people on this continent have risen from the ranks by their own industry and exertions, and knowing this, have no sympathy with the indolent and slothful, who need not expect success here any more than at home.

The next place we visited was Toronto. This city is a very neat clean town, and beautifully laid out, one of the streets extending away into the country, bearing the name of Young Street; it is *thirty-six miles* long, and is probably the longest street in existence. Many of the buildings are of stone, and all have the appearance of comfort, stability, and good taste. We went to visit some friends at a place called Everton, ten miles from Guelph. We drove in a carriage and pair from Guelph to Everton and back, the cost being only twelve shillings and sixpence, driver included, being the cheapest drive ever we had in any country. We just stepped in upon our friends unannounced; they did not know that we were coming, in fact they had never seen any of us. They gave us a warm and hearty welcome, and the old lady of the house, the ancient Christian friend of our revered father, wept for joy. We found her sitting with her open Bible before her: she had changed her country but not her religion. We had lighted on a Bethel in the Western world. Of course all the neighbours had to be brought in to see the strangers from Scotland, and we had to give all the news to every fresh comer. Thirty-six years ago our friends settled in this part of the country, which at that time was covered with "bush," the trees being hardwood, chiefly beech and maple, of large size. They came hither poor enough, but are now owners of a large tract of country, and are in circumstances of comparative affluence: such is the usual result of perseverance and honest toil in the New World. The land is of excellent quality, and almost anything can be grown; very different from the poor soil we saw in Lower Canada, where pine trees prevail—sure indication of a poor country. When we took our departure there was quite a crowd of villagers round the carriage, waiting to say goodbye to us, it being an unusual sight here to see travellers from the "old country." We returned to Toronto by the "Wild Cat" train, so called from its irregular movements, being a mixed train of passengers and goods. It was past one A.M. when we reached our hotel, although we had left Guelph about seven, our progress having thus been at the rate of only nine miles per hour or thereby. But this is just a specimen of the kind of railways one meets with in Canada —bad rails, bad carriages, and slow trains.

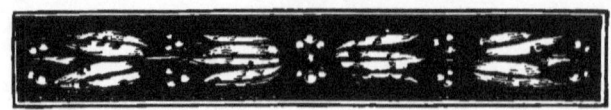

CHAPTER XII.

Niagara Falls.

WE came by steamer from Toronto, on Lake Ontario, *via* Niagara River, to Lewiston, and thence per rail to the Falls. About two miles below the Falls there is a fine suspension bridge, over which the railway to Chicago is carried, while close upon the Falls there is a new wire rope bridge for carriage and foot passengers, so slim, that, when the wind blows hard, it shakes like an aspen leaf, and therefore people are not allowed to cross on such occasions. The view of the Falls from the centre of this aerial bridge is most exquisite. It takes some time to realize the stupendous scene upon which you are looking. At every turn it is presented in a different aspect; now the roar is louder, now lower, now the spray dances up and touches the clouds, then the sun shining through the mist creates a gorgeous rainbow, which spans from side to side of the pouring foam, planting its Canadian limb in the deep green of the vast volume of water ever pouring over the land side of the Horse Shoe Fall. The worst of it is you cannot contemplate quietly the greatness of the scene before you by reason of the numerous photographing touters, who importune you to be permitted to photograph you on the spot, Falls and all; or who wish to inform you, forsooth, that the rainbow is now visible; or who want you to ascend here or descend there, or buy this or look at that:—everything for the almighty dollar. The force and power of this tremendous body of water, if utilized, would make the fortune of a Manchester or a Dundee, a Philadelphia or a Pittsburg. A paper manufactory near the brink of the fall is the only attempt to turn to account this wondrous force. It is surprising that some pushing Yankee has not already turned it to greater account. The mightiest works that man could erect, so far from impairing the splendour of the scene, would merely serve to show the insignificance of man and all his works, compared with this vast and unparalleled phenomenon of nature.

While viewing the Falls, a notable, and from this point almost total eclipse of the sun took place, of which we enjoyed a most beautiful view from the Canadian side; it so happening that Niagara was one of the best places in the whole world for observing this eclipse. The obscuration was greatest at 5·45 P.M., when nearly nine-tenths of the sun's disc was hid from view. Altogether, the magnificent Falls, the rainbow produced by the ascending spray, rendered visible and invisible alternately as the obscuration of the sun increased and decreased, and the darkness of the eclipse itself, combined to form a scene of impressive and awful grandeur, seldom witnessed, and impossible adequately to describe.

We also visited Goat Island, a scene of romantic beauty, and had exquisite views of the falls and rapids from the various points there. The trees and shrubs on the island have been planted by the hand of nature, and are in beautiful and primitive confusion,—surpassing in charm all art. Rocks appear as if tumbled amidst the roaring rapids in endless variety of form; little verdure-clad islands dotted amidst the rushing torrents; trees growing out of openings in the solid rock,—presenting altogether a wonderful and most entrancing scene.

We went under the fall on the Canadian side, at Termination Point. For this purpose we crossed over the River Niagara, and were rigged out in tarpaulins and sou'-westers, as a protection from the drifting spray. A black man accompanied us as guide; but so great was the thunder of the falls that we could not hear each other speak. The projecting portion of Table Rock, from which a fine view of the falls was formerly obtained, has been blown down by order of the British Government, a crack rendering it unsafe. Above us was the water pouring down right over our heads, the fall here being 160 feet. We could only remain a few minutes under the watery veil, owing to the spray beating on our faces with stifling force. We also visited some of the battle-fields situated round about the falls. The chief of these is Lundy's Lane, where one thousand English and as many Americans lie buried, although the battle lasted only four hours. There is neither a stone nor any other mark to show where so many bodies lie of friends and foes.

We left Niagara exceedingly well pleased with our visit, bidding farewell with reluctance to the grand and magnificent scene. The hotel where we stayed, Cataract House, is a large new building, and very nicely done up; and we afterwards regretted that we had not prolonged our stay at this delightful, cool, and most charming spot.

CHAPTER XIII.

Chicago.

FROM Niagara we proceeded to Chicago, distant 513 miles; fare, first-class, 15½ dollars, about a penny per mile, per Great Western of Canada and Illinois Central Railroads. The carriages and road are much superior to those of the Grand Trunk, and nearly as smooth as our own home lines. Part of our way lay through the finest land in Canada. Some of the hardwood forests are still remaining, being left for fuel, but they are getting gradually displaced by the cultivation of the fields. In some of the fields the stumps of the trees are still in the ground, being allowed to remain until they rot. The land in this district, we were told, was worth £10 an acre, and was about the same value whether cleared or not, if contiguous to the line of rail, the wood being of sufficient value in that case to pay for the clearing. All that appears to be wanting in this country is, that it should be more adequately peopled by Scotch farmers and labourers, combined with moderate capital. Doubtless it would then soon become one of the finest agricultural lands on the face of the earth. A man with a large family of sons would, with health and strength, soon make himself comfortable and comparatively independent in a country such as this, even if blessed with little means at the start.

As we proceeded westward on our way to Chicago we noticed a change in the nature of the land. Beyond Detroit the hills, vales, and trees, characteristic of Canadian scenery, begin to disappear, and plains covered with grass come into view. On some of these plains nothing interrupts the view for miles and miles together. On the borders of Lake Michigan stands the city of Chicago, the capital of the Western Prairies. This city is admittedly the most go-a-head in the whole Union. Thirty years ago a small village only stood here; now it has a population of 350,000, and covers a space of about seven miles long by four miles wide. It is laid out in handsome streets; one of them, Wabash Avenue, running the whole length of the city—seven miles—without interruption. Street cars ply both lengthways and crossways at regular intervals, and 'buses run besides on the principal streets and avenues. The streets are all laid with wooden blocks, in the same way as ours are laid with stone. This kind of causewaying, though not so durable, is a great deal more comfortable for the horses, and more noiseless than the stone blocks. The sidewalks were originally laid with wood as well as the roadway. They are also planted with cotton-wood trees, poplars, &c., but in some parts of the city the wooden sidewalk is being relaid with granite stones, some of which are of an enormous size, measuring ten feet by five feet, and about nine inches in thickness, even the curb-stones being about six feet by three feet by four inches in thickness.

Most of the houses are of wood, but nearly all the new buildings are of brick, faced with a beautiful white lime-stone found in the immediate neighbourhood, and most of the houses are of elegant designs. From the rapid growth of the city, some of the edifices are rendered unsuitable for what they were originally intended; this is what has given rise to the extraordinary practice of house moving, for which this city is so famous. No sooner is a better house wanted in any given location than the old erection is put upon wheels or rollers and drawn off to a more suburban site. We saw a number of houses being pulled through the streets in this way, and many more being raised to a higher level, the people living in them the while, and coolly pursuing their ordinary avocations, undisturbed by the curious transition their shells were undergoing. Chicago, when founded, was laid out without any regard to its future importance, and no provision being made for its drainage, it has been found necessary to raise the whole city some five to ten feet above its original level. The mode of house raising is as follows:—Beams of wood are placed under the foundations lengthways and crossways, and then scores of screw-jacks are placed under the timbers; men are placed at the jacks, give a turn of the screw simultaneously, and away the house goes up, and so on at each turn of the screw till the requisite height is attained. The better class of houses, and the public buildings, are of limestone, some of the stores being most elegant and extensive. One store, the chief dry goods emporium in the city, had a palatial appearance, the retail department being fitted up with Parisian regard to taste and refinement.

Chicago is beautifully situated for commerce, and it is this that makes it the chief city of the north-west. The trade in grain and lumber (or timber) is probably the greatest in the world. We saw numbers of the grain warehouses or "elevators" as they are called. The grain is brought in from all directions by sixteen or eighteen different lines of rails, and the mode of discharging the trucks is very interesting. The trucks are brought alongside the elevators, and the end of a wooden spout being introduced, containing an endless chain of buckets, the grain is quickly raised up the spout to any elevation desired. In loading, the vessels come alongside of the elevator, and the grain is spouted into the hold by several spouts at one time, so that a vessel of a thousand tons burden can be loaded in the short space of three hours. On the banks of the river there are about twenty of these elevators, capable of containing a million quarters of grain.

The drainage of the city runs into Chicago river, and as the latter is nearly level with the lake, there is scarcely any current, so that a nuisance is the result; but works are in course of construction for deepening the river, and producing a scour to carry the drainage right down the Mississippi. In consequence of the land being so level and so little above the elevation of the river, it was found necessary to raise the grades of the city to the extent of about five feet and upwards, to secure proper drainage. The cost of all this has been very great, but the people of Chicago are not accustomed to stick at trifles.

They have other important works which we visited, one of the most interesting being their water-works, which we reached by special steamer, placed at our service by our hospitable entertainer, Mr L. In this pleasant way we reached the "Crib," an immense octagonal box of about fifty feet diameter and seventy feet long, which, having been built on shore, and made water-tight, was then floated out two miles off into the lake, and sunk in a depth of water of about forty feet. Stone masonry was then built inside so as to sink it some nineteen feet deeper into the mud at the bottom of the lake. An iron tube of ten feet in diameter was fitted inside the masonry with proper openings to admit the water. This tube is joined to the shore by a brick tunnel six feet under the bed of the lake, and is a work of no ordinary engineering difficulty. At the shore end there are three powerful engines which pump the water to the top of a lofty tower, whence the city is supplied by gravitation. The water thus obtained is always pure, and free from the wash of the waves, which, if it were drawn from nearer the shore, would interfere with its purity.

The river, which intersects the city, has been deepened and fitted for carrying on an extensive commerce. Numerous swing bridges span the river, and are continually being opened to allow the shipping to pass and repass, laden with grain and lumber to and from the various ports on the Great Lakes. There is also a tunnel underneath the river to relieve the bridges, they being insufficient for the vast concourse of foot passengers and carriages of every description, continually coming and going at all points. It is proposed to construct a number of these tunnels, and we doubt not but that they will be made, for if the Americans see that any engineering work will *pay*, they are sure to go on and carry it out.

Situated also upon the banks of the river are the pork-curing establishments, pork-curing being one of the most important trades of Chicago. The houses where the pigs are manipulated are all constructed on the same principle. An inclined plane or stair leads up to the top of the building, up which the animals are driven. On arrival there they are despatched, plunged into a boiling vat, scraped, cut up and pickled. The whole process occupies about five minutes for each pig, and we were informed that at some of the establishments as many as five thousand will be packed daily during the season. The lumber yards are also situated on the banks of the river. There are a large number of these yards, and a very extensive trade is done. The value of the timber exported, not including that used in Chicago, amounts to £2,000,000 sterling annually. If all this timber were loaded in the usual manner upon railway waggons, it would have a length of about four thousand miles, or sufficient to reach from Shetland to Chicago.

But the most wonderful branch of business carried on here is to be seen at the Stock Market, which covers a space of 350 acres, 100 acres being floored over with wood, laid out in streets, and railed off into pens and sheds for cattle, sheep, and pigs. Of the latter as many as four million have been sold in one year at this market. The total of stock which annually changes hands here amounts to nearly £10,000,000 sterling. For the transaction of this enormous business in live stock, a bank, hotel, and exchange have been erected on the spot. In order to obtain water for the cattle, two gigantic Artesian wells have been sunk, the first 1032 feet in depth, yielding 6500 gallons daily. This having been found insufficient, another well was commenced, and not till it had been sunk to a depth of 1100 feet was water found. At length, when despairing of success, a subterranean river was struck, and water burst up in a powerful rush. On plumbing, it was found that the subterranean river had a depth of eight feet, with a strong current flowing from south-west to north-east. The direction of the current was proved by the plumb line remaining perfectly perpendicular till it reached the water, when it was carried off to one side. The pipe of this well is nine inches diameter at the bottom, and six inches at the top, and the well produces 600,000 gallons of water daily, sufficient to supply, by gravitation, the whole Stock Market. Strangest of all, these two wells, sunk within a few feet of one another, produce two entirely different kinds of water, the one being impregnated with sulphur, while the other contains iron, both thus being of valuable medicinal qualities. We were indebted to the able manager, Mr. Sherman, for these particulars. He also shewed us some majestic specimens of the native Illinois oxen, some of which weighed 3700, 3600, and 3500 lbs. each. They were extremely handsome, quiet, and docile animals, and were in very fine condition, the average weight of a hundred head of such oxen being 3200 lbs., completely casting into the shade our biggest prize oxen. There was also a specimen of the wild Texas cattle, the value of which in their own native herds is only a few dollars each.

We visited a large number of other places of interest in this fine city, including the Opera House, which is a handsome building. Surrounded as Chicago is, she will no doubt rise to be the first or second city in the Union, for she has everything calculated to increase her wealth,—magnificent land, coal, copper, and iron near at hand, together with water and rail conveyance, while the people are perhaps the most go-a-head and energetic in America. We were greatly disappointed with the hotel accommodation in Chicago, which was about the worst we met with in the States, Omaha always excepted, and quite unworthy of the city. We shall never forget the kindness of our friend Mr. L., who insisted we should take up our abode under his hospitable roof, and we were only too glad to bid adieu to the mosquitoes and dirt of the famed Sherman House. Chicago is noted for its fast trotting horses, the wide, level, straight, and withal softly paved streets, being eminently suitable for the rapid movements of the crowds of spidery vehicles which are there to be seen coursing along at the extraordinary pace of fifteen to twenty miles an hour. Ever attentive to strangers, a friend waited upon us one evening and gave us a drive out in his racing gig, when we were whirled along at the incredible pace of a mile in two minutes and forty-five seconds, a rate exceeding that at which most American railway trains usually travel.

CHAPTER XIV.

American Churches.

IN the city of Chicago there are about one hundred and twenty churches, many of them handsome stone buildings, erected at great cost. We saw one wooden church taking a stroll through the city: it was being removed to a different site for a new suburban congregation who had just purchased it. Another large church of brick we saw which had been removed and re-erected, having been replaced by a costly stone building—the latter belonging to the Baptist denomination—was the largest in the city, and was capable of containing two thousand persons.

The American churches are much more comfortable than those in the old country, and are, so far as we could judge, even better attended. In every church there is a handsome organ, with usually three or four or more paid singers, in addition to a large volunteer choir. The service generally commences with a beautiful anthem by the choir— a morning hymn—appropriate and solemnizing. A short prayer follows. The subsequent singing is generally joined in by the audience with ardour and cultivated taste,—a vast improvement on the barbarous music of many of our Scotch churches, where a pious horror of organs prevails, and piety and discordant howling are supposed to be synonymous.

When will we in Scotland get rid of the notion that the organ is a sinful institution? When will we take a lesson from the birds, the trees, the waterfalls? They all sing their hymns of praise and the trees "clap their hands" on Sundays as well as Saturdays; and why should we not bring the best of everything, the tongue of cedar and of brass, as well as the human voice, to make a joyful noise to God our Maker? "The earth is the Lord's, and the fulness thereof," and why should we not lay all on His altar? Away with the narrowness, the bigotry, the ignorance that would exclude from God's house instrumental music, and condemn us to the untutored discordant sounds too long prevalent in our churches. Praise God with the heart, and with the understanding; apply your understanding to the creatures of creation; lend all to give glory to God in the highest; He is equally the maker of the timber and the metal of the organ as of the human frame. Why, why should there be thus constant cant about organs? Let us get the best of everything to praise and magnify His great name, who is the universal Creator.

The preaching in America seemed to us as superior to ours as the singing was. Short practical discourses, delivered with point and energy; discourses applicable to the work of every-day life, not dry doctrinal disquisitions manufactured in the study and fit only for the book-shelf. American ministers are men, and don't pretend to be anything but men; they mingle in every-day life, and in the pulpit, or rather on the platform—for pulpits there are none—they speak to the people in the language of the day, and not in the time-worn, meaningless phrases of past ages, such as we too often hear repeated Sabbath after Sabbath at home, with the unvarying whine with which some eminent saint fifty years ago disfigured his delivery. In America at all events, every man is himself, and that is saying a good deal. The pews and passages of the churches are usually laid with carpets, the seats and backs are sloped and padded, wide and easy, not like the narrow uncomfortable boxes that are so common in our own churches. The Sunday school-rooms are generally below the church, and are also nicely carpeted, and divided into rooms and compartments, each class with its own separate division. They are also accompanied in their singing by an organ or harmonium; and the whole arrangements are attractive and interesting to the crowds of children who are there instructed by bands of enthusiastic teachers, devoted to their most interesting and most useful work. The Sabbath afternoons are generally devoted to the Sunday school; the church services being held morning and evening, another vast improvement on our Scottish system.

CHAPTER XV.

Omaha—an Upset.

HAVING finished the sight-seeing in Chicago, we took our tickets for San Francisco, California, distant by the Pacific Railway 2393 miles—a pretty big jump on one ticket, even for America. Over mountains, valleys, rivers, and prairies—or pa-rairies, as the word is here pronounced—lies the iron road. To the west of Chicago the land is of the richest prairie character, producing, where cultivated, abundant crops, chiefly of Indian corn; but vast tracts are here lying untouched by the plough, covered with long waving natural grass, withering and dying with each returning year, given up to everlasting solitude. Only here and there appears a cultivated patch and a solitary immigrant's wooden hut; and then for miles and miles the only living thing visible may be the fire-fly dancing as the shades of evening draw in, lighting up with fairy flashes the lonely plains. What a magnificent country this for the pent-up millions of our sadly over-populated country, huddled together as they are in narrow closes, courts, and lanes, while boundless space here lies unoccupied; a splendid heritage for the great Creator's ill-fed, ill-clad children. Let emigrants form themselves into societies of one to two hundred, with their doctor, their minister, their schoolmaster, their baker, their joiner, their blacksmith, and come in bodies to settle in villages and townships in these glorious prairies, and they will find themselves in a new world,—a heaven on earth, compared with the poverty and squalor of our large towns, or the penury and struggles of our country districts, where labour is lifelong and incessant, even for the barest and meanest necessities, and rest or repose only in the workhouse or the churchyard. Here there will be labour and toil and hardship no doubt to begin with, but the reward will come, and perseverance will assuredly bring comfort, plenty, and repose for the evening of life.

Musing thus, as we speeded through this rich and splendid country, a thunderstorm overtook us, the only one we encountered on the American continent. Dark and fearful grew the troubled sky, and then burst forth flashes of sheet and forked lightning, terribly grand, while the peals of thunder rolled high above the rattle of the train, and the rain descended in bucketfuls.

> "Hark! the deep tremendous voice
> Of awful thunder roars!
> The tempest howls around.
> Away; ah let us fly!
> Flashes of livid flame dart thro' the air,
> And from the bursting clouds the flood
> In sundry torrents pours.
> Heaven protect us!
> Dreadful rage the winds; the sky is all in flames.
> Oh, what horror!
> Peal on peal, with fearful crash.
> Convulsing heaven, the thunder rolls!
> O God! O God!
> Unto its deep foundations
> The solid globe is shook."

After a journey of some twenty-seven hours we arrived at Council Bluffs (so called from being the spot where the American Commissioners formerly held their palavers with the Indian Chiefs), where our way lay across the River Missouri. It was midnight, and in a thunderstorm. We had to get into omnibuses and descend by a rascally road to the bed of the river, and cross by a rickety ferry-boat. Such a night as this had been chosen for the experiment of a new landing. With difficulty the omnibuses were dragged, with many a jolt, on board, and at last we got under weigh for the other side. Meanwhile the miserable glimmering petroleum lamps went out, and all was darkness. The passage was dismal, and rendered all the more so by the evil prognostications of the doubtful-looking characters who were our fellow-passengers. We would never get across, they said; there was not water enough; we would be left high and dry in the middle of the Missouri all night; even if we got across we would not be able to land, and, if landed, the driver did not know the new road, and would be sure to overturn the vehicle. Such was the ominous conversation in the dark conveyance as the steamer groped its way over the stream. At length we reached the opposite shore with a jerk, and, the river being low, we had a long distance to traverse over its muddy bed, the road being composed of branches of trees laid in the soft clay. One man with a solitary lamp preceded the string of omnibuses along this abominable swamp. We saw the lights of Omaha "City" in the distance, and were congratulating ourselves that our misery would soon be ended; but alas, still worse remained behind, for suddenly the omnibus gave a lurch, and we were pitched into each other's arms! Then came a cry to get out, and out we scrambled, ankle deep in dirt, amongst the feet of the horses of the succeeding conveyance. No sooner had we escaped than our vehicle, horses and all, disappeared heels overhead down an embankment into the slush and blackness. Wading through the ruts and hillocks of soft clay, we made our way at last to the wretched hotel, where we told our tale; but the upset of an omnibus appeared in these parts to occasion little surprise and less concern. With difficulty could we procure a lamp from our callous host for the extrication of the *débris*. Our baggage, for the most part, we had to abandon for the time to its fate, only securing with difficulty a precious valise, containing our cash; but next morning, fortunately, we recovered the remainder of our goods and chattels all right, the wet and dirt excepted. Happily no one was hurt, only the omnibus and harness destroyed; as for the horses, they appeared to be accustomed to that sort of thing, poor brutes, and to every other kind of hardship. When one goes out West he must be prepared to rough it. We had now got a tasting of the pleasures of Western travel. We had heard of the comforts of Western hotels, but till we came to Omaha we had not experienced them. The comforts of the hotel were on a par with those of the approach to it. Dilapidation, filth, and abominations indescribable, were the order of the day, or rather of that dismal night.

Next morning, after a wretched night upon the hard bed, we found our boots, all wet and muddy, as we had left them. After repeated calls, at length a lazy Negro appeared, but it was not his duty to clean boots or to carry them to the boot-black. He would deliver the message to that functionary, that was his duty. After waiting and despairing, we had to do porter's duty ourselves; and carrying our boots to the sanctum of the artist in question, found him to be a huge black man plying his art as if to the tune of the Old Hundred, oblivious of our urgent call. The Negro *gentleman*, whose duty was *not* to carry boots, introduced us as the "man" who wanted to have his boots blacked. At last the business was accomplished, but only in that slovenly fashion in which the Negro race seem to perform all their work.

CHAPTER XVI.

Across the Prairies to California.

OMAHA City is the eastern terminus of the Pacific Railway, and it was from this station that we resumed our journey to California. We secured a section of one of Pulman's Palace Sleeping Cars, and then had time to look around us. These cars are a great institution in America, and are very extensively used on all the lines. In their internal arrangements they resemble the cabin of a ship, having two rows of berths, situated the one above the other. In the daytime the sleeping accommodation is folded up and put out of sight, and in a twinkling the carriage is converted into an elegant drawing-room car. Some of these cars are divided into sections, each section containing four berths, suitable for a family party. Such carriages will hold about forty persons, and in the morning ladies and gentlemen wash and dress themselves promiscuously together with primitive simplicity. One or two black men attend to the making down and folding up of the berths; they will also black your boots, for which the charge is twenty-five cents, or equal to about ninepence sterling! Bootblacking, like hair-cutting, is a high and expensive art here. At a roadside station half way to California, in the desert, two darkie artists proffered their services in this line at the moderate charge of one shilling sterling. On my declining their services upon economical grounds, the grinning black eyed me from top to toe, and remarked with twinkling humour, " Ah, I guessed you could not afford it!"

For about two hundred miles beyond Omaha City the land is of excellent prairie character, but is very little cultivated as yet. The value originally was one and a quarter dollars per acre, but adjoining the railway it now fetches from five to twenty dollars an acre, according to quality, &c. As we proceeded farther on our route we found the soil get gradually poorer, till it ended in sterile alkali-covered sand, where nothing will grow. At certain intervals the Railway Company have established eating-houses, where passengers can obtain food. We found the quality on the whole bad, and all three meals, breakfast, dinner, and supper, were almost identical, viz., tea, buffalo steaks, antelope chops, sweet potatoes, and boiled Indian corn, with hoe cakes and syrup *ad nauseam.*

We saw a few Indians on our way west, but they are gradually getting fewer in numbers. The United States Government have allotted to them certain " Reservations," in compensation for their hunting grounds taken from them in the westward march of the white man. Unfortunately the Commissioners sent by the Government to carry out these Indian treaties too often betray their trust, and apply to their own enrichment the funds voted to the Indians for the purpose of setting them up to pursue the peaceful occupations of civilized life. Seeds that will not grow, implements that will not work, are foisted upon the unsuspecting children of the prairie, and their pensions pocketed by the unprincipled carpet-baggers from Washington. The poor Indian's patience becomes exhausted, and his family famishing, he rises in his wrath, and white massacres are the result. More troops are sent west, and the Indians are hunted to the death. Such, too often, is the history of the so-called " Indian wars." Many of the chiefs are men of honour and hospitality, receiving the visits of the Commissioners with dignity, and willing to adhere to their treaties faithfully if only the representatives of the Government would carry out honestly the instructions they receive.

This year the Government, which means well by the Indians, were its intentions properly carried out by its representatives, has voted the sum of five millions of dollars for their amelioration and civilization, and it also supports a society composed of all religious denominations, which is actively and successfully engaged in establishing schools and churches among them. The success achieved in Canada under the British Government, in the complete Christianization of our Indian subjects there, shows what can be done in this direction. But the great drawback in the case of the United States is the frequent change of officials which accompanies every change of Government. It too often follows that the Indian Commissioner looks not so much to the improvement of the Indians under his charge, as to the securing of his own pecuniary interest by fair play or foul in the brief period during which his official reign may last.

We passed a number of small forts erected by the Government, and garrisoned by American troops, for the purpose of keeping down the Indians, and preserving the peace generally amongst the diggers, ranchmen, and adventurers of these western wilds. The poor fellows eagerly clutched at the old newspapers thrown to them from the train. At Sherman, which is 8235 feet above the level of the sea, we saw herds of antelopes and numbers of the little prairie dog. Here we dropt several hunters, some even from Liverpool, come hither all the way for sport and excitement. The country for hundreds of miles on to Echo Canyon is a dreary wilderness, the surface of the ground being covered with alkali, and is never likely to be of any use for cultivation. If minerals are found, it will help to increase the population; at present confined chiefly to the tented " cities," springing up around the railway stations, which depend for their commerce upon the passengers and the workmen upon the line. Wood is the fuel principally used on the Pacific Railroad; but at several points we saw signs of coal cropping out near the surface by the side of the line. At Echo Canyon, 993 miles from Omaha city, we passed through a deep, wild, rocky gorge, where the red stone boulders are, to appearance, from four to eight hundred feet in height, with scenery wild and weird. It was at this point that Brigham Young stationed his riflemen, and successfully defied the United States troops. The Americans are fond of startling names: here we passed through an opening in the gorge called the Devil's Gate; and a curious rock formation on the mountain they have named the Devil's Slide!

CHAPTER XVII.

Salt Lake City: Mormonism.

AT Uintah Station you may, if you please, leave the train and go down thirty-two miles per stage, and visit the famous Salt Lake City—the New Jerusalem, the Modern Zion—where dwells and reigns that well-to-do apostle, with fifty wives, Brigham Young. The ride was simply horrible,—the heat, the dust, the jolting, awful! There is no made road. Over water-courses, river-beds, fords, hill, dale—just as they come—you dash away, neck or nothing! How the stage did not tumble upside down we cannot fancy. On gently hinting at such a contingency, our Jehu merely remarked,—"I guess it takes a deal to capsize them things;" and, cracking his whip, bang, bang we went. The country here is covered with salt, which, in the moonlight, glistens like snow, and blowing into nose, eyes, and mouth, parches, irritates, and torments.

On the way we passed various little Mormon settlements, wherever a mountain stream gave them the means of irrigating their little gardens; for without irrigation nothing will grow in this bleak, scorched, barren, and seemingly God-forsaken country. At one of these villages we stopped to refresh in the Mormon roadside inn. The landlord had been twenty years there, and had three wives, or rather slaves.

They served the guests in a woe-begone, down-cast, spiritless way, to miserable, uneatable fare, for which we had to contend with the legion of flies that hovered over and alighted in tormenting crowds upon the table. Only we got the bill to pay all to ourselves, and salt enough bills are in Salt Lake City.

After some five hours of cruel jolting we approached the City of the Saints. Outside the city is a sulphur spring, from which wells forth a stream, green and pungent. Here a certain Gentile physician, named Dr. Robertson, had established sulphur baths for the cure of the saints (whose faith, by the way, admits of no cure but by the laying on of hands). Whether for this transgression, or for some other quarrel, it was said that the doctor had rendered himself obnoxious to the Mormons. As the story goes, the hierarchy of the Mormon Church includes a certain order of destroying angels, whose office it is to execute the church's decrees. To the tender mercies of this host the doctor, it is said, was duly consigned. A case requiring his professional attendance on a certain night, he was called into the city, and, returning to his sulphur spring, after having discharged his professional duty, a bullet sent him to his long home. The hand that fired the shot was never known; at all events the deed was never punished. Some years ago, as another story goes, before the days of the railroad, a party of emigrants were wending their dreary way across these arid plains to California—a six months' journey of immense hardship and fatigue, of which we saw evidence in the bleaching skeletons of horses and cattle strewn along the highway—a journey this to which not only the cattle, but a proportion of the goldhunters themselves regularly succumbed. What the Amorite, the Hittite, and the Perizzite were to the Children of Israel, the Gentiles are to the Mormons. Pretending friendship, they waylaid this particular band of weary wayworn emigrants, and professing to give advice as to the Indians, and how to avoid their attacks, they thus spied out the strength of the Gentile train. Disguised as Indians, they afterwards fell upon them at another point, and ruthlessly murdered in cold blood the whole band, men, women, and children. Such were the tales that were told us as we approached this New Jerusalem.

The walls were now in view, and such walls! Only a small bit remains. They were of common mud, and have already crumbled into dust, emblematical of the system within, which happily is already tottering to its fall. Brigham Young is the king, judge, pope, priest, and president of Mormondom, and he clearly means to make the business pay.

The church and state are one concern here, and Brigham is the treasurer; and being the prophet of the Lord, he is above suspicion, and needs no auditors for his accounts, except it may be the worthy twelve apostles. The new arrivals are appointed locations by the twelve, and have to settle the price with the prophet, who also condescends to receive annually a tenth of the earnings of the faithful for " the good of the church." Besides being a preacher, Brigham is tax-gatherer, storekeeper, printer, publisher, flour-miller, and, as we were informed, keeper of a grog-shop. Having fifty wives, partly temporal, partly spiritual, and all this business besides, he must be acknowledged to be an industrious man. In fact the beehive is his coat of arms; a large one surmounting harem No. 1, which is called the Beehive House. The other and larger is called the Lion House; " The Lion of the Lord " being another of Brigham's modest titles. The Tabernacle is the chief building in the place, and is probably the largest in America. It is said to seat 10,000 persons, a gallery being in contemplation to accommodate 6000 more. In shape it is like a gigantic dish-cover, is surmounted by a flag-staff, and is so constructed that the vast congregation can disperse in three minutes' time. Here Brigham holds forth on Sundays. His sermons are always printed in his own newspaper, " The Deseret News." The gospel, according to Brigham, appears to amount very much to this,—" Work hard and pay your tithes."

Here is a sample of this new gospel, extracted from an address which he delivered on 7th April last:—" If the people called 'Latter-Day Saints' do not become one in temporal things as they are in spiritual things, they will not build up the Zion of God. The co-operative movement is a stepping-stone. We say to the people, take advantage of it. You will find that if the people hearken to the counsel that is given them, it will not be long before the hats, caps, bonnets, boots and shoes, pants, vests, and underclothing of this entire community will be made in our midst. I am tired of this everlasting ding-dong about fashions. If I happen to have a coat on that is not what is called fashionable, some of my wives will be sure to say to me, 'Husband,' or 'Mr. President, may I give this away?' or, 'I wish it were out of sight, it is not fashionable.' But I do not care for the fashions. I do not care who wears a bonnet that is six feet above the head behind, twelve feet in front, or that fits close to the crown of the head, or whether it is three straws thrown over the head, with ribbons to them." Such is the gospel, according to Brigham. This system of co-operation was a plan adopted to starve out the Gentiles— that is, all who would not pay their tithes. The Mormon storekeepers were therefore ordained to adopt a sign over their premises to let the faithful know who were Mormon traders and who were not. And this was the sign—

" HOLINESS TO THE LORD!"
(A representation of the All-seeing Eye.)
" ZION'S CO-OPERATIVE COMMERCIAL INSTITUTION."
" Dry Goods, Wholesale and Retail.—(Boots and Butter.)"

This blasphemous signboard stares at you all through Mormondom.

Great Salt Lake City, as the Mormons call it, is simply a big village of some 20,000 inhabitants. It is three miles square; the streets 100 to 120 feet wide, unpaved and uncausewayed. Little streams of water run down each side, and irrigate, as required, the little Mormon gardens. The houses are chiefly of wood or unburnt brick, and are of a poor character, but mostly surrounded by little gardens. The best houses belong chiefly to the apostles and prophets, who appear to look out for the best share of the loaves and fishes, as well as of wives. In fact, before you can have any office in the Mormon church, you must have a goodly estate, and at least three wives, and before you can be an apostle, you must have six or eight at least; but ten or twelve is considered more respectable, while the prophet himself sets the example with fifty or thereby; but it is shrewdly suspected that in reality his reverence has lost count and reckoning some time ago both of wives and children.

"Brigham's Block" is the chief block in the city, and covers ten acres. The walls enclose the two harems aforesaid; the "Deseret" Store; the Deseret Newspaper Office; the Tithing Office; a special schoolhouse for his numerous family, his garden, and a separate cottage, occupied it is said by Mrs. Brigham senior, now too old and ugly for either the Beehive or the Lion House. The Tabernacle and the foundations of a temple, which is to vie with Solomon's in splendour when finished, if ever, occupies another ten acre block contiguous to Brigham's. On the sacred stones of the temple we were forbidden to tread. These two are the best blocks in the city, and occupy the most commanding situation. The Mormon rulers deny allegiance to the United States, refuse to pay taxes, and buy up, it is said, the judges sent down from Washington to administer the laws. The decisions in the law courts, therefore, as well as the gospel, and everything else, are according to Brigham.

It formerly was no light matter accordingly to differ either in religion or politics from this potent "Lion of the Lord" and his twelve apostles; but now the United States have got a camp of soldiers within a couple of miles of the city, and their artillery commands Brigham's block, which formerly was the rallying point for the saintly soldiers of the prophet. The Mormons, being the modern "chosen people," are fond of Bible names; having a tabernacle, a temple, a new Jerusalem, a lion of the Lord, and angels of the destroying order. They have also a River Jordan, which flows fast by this modern Zion into the new Dead Sea—the Great Salt Lake. Formerly, we were told, it was no uncommon thing to find over night dead Gentiles in this Jordan, but how they came there usually remained a mystery. Now, however, since the establishment of Camp Douglas these mysteries are fewer.

The Great Salt Lake is 100 miles long by 35 miles wide, and is so highly impregnated with salt that, like the Dead Sea of Palestine, it contains little or no life. It is 4000 feet above the level of the sea, and is distant from the city about eleven miles. Its surroundings are wild and weird, and on its banks in hot weather a thick incrustation of salt is deposited. Of course vegetation is impossible.

The situation of Salt Lake City has been deservedly praised, and its selection shows that even if Brigham had not the vision from heaven which he pretends to have had at Pulpit Rock, he is yet a shrewd, clever man. The valley is surrounded by the Rocky Mountains, rising 2000 to 4000 feet, from the tops of which the everlasting snows send down during the dry season delightful fertilizing streams of snow water, which, running down the sides of the streets, irrigate the gardens and little farms. But for these streams no being could exist in these barren, sterile, salt-parched, rainless valleys. Aided by these streams, the inhabitants, after much labour, raise crops of Indian corn, sargund or sugar cane, peaches, pears, apples, melons, grapes, a little cotton, &c.; but the poor are obliged to work very hard, and, we were told, are seldom able to procure any butcher meat at all. The Mormons represent it as a land flowing with milk and honey; but, as we were told by one of the citizens, the milk flows at the rate of 2s. 3d. per gallon, and the honey at 3s. per pound. Such is the Paradise to which the Mormons are induced to emigrate by the specious bunkum of the Mormon evangelists; and yet, season after season, consignments of these poor creatures are arriving, like dumb driven cattle, from Germany, Wales, England, and even from Scotland.

All does not go well with Brigham however. The sons of Joseph, the first prophet, have grown up, and they are preaching a crusade against the grand pillar of the faith—Bigamy, or Brighamy,—and this in the very citadel of Mormonism. The American Government also have at last had their attention aroused to this blot upon their flag, and are now giving their attention to its removal. The railway will shortly be completed to the very doors of the Temple, by which the Gentiles will pour in, and by their open jeers probably assist in breaking up this unholy community.

Brigham is sixty-eight years of age, and it may be that he may have to choose in another vision another place of refuge, far from civilization, for his peculiar institution, or rather mission, or, as some say, trade. One of the Sandwich Islands is supposed to be the direction in which the prophetic vision will next tend, unless indeed the seer sees fit to retire from business altogether, and rest on his laurels in this happy hunting ground of ours—in this our dear native land, where dethroned monarchs from every clime find a shelter and a home.

Our experiences in the City of the Saints were anything but agreeable. The thermometer stood 118° in the sun, and walking was impossible. We therefore hired a one-horse carriage, and for three quarters of an hour's use thereof we were charged the moderate sum of 21s., which, as a special favour, we got modified to 10s. 6d. Everything was at ransom prices, and bad.

By day there was the plague of the heat, and the plague of the locusts, and the plague of the myriad flies. By night there was the plague of the croaking frogs without, and the worse plague of a certain flattish, oval, brown-coloured insect within. We therefore bade adieu to Salt Lake City without regret, glad to escape in safety from this modern City of the Plain.

CHAPTER XVIII.

On the Prairies again.

WE left Salt Lake City at five o'clock in the morning, on our return to Uintah station, in order to resume our journey to California, thankful that we had escaped without serious harm from the doubtful hospitalities and horrors of Mormondom. We partook of breakfast at a Mormon wayside inn, and were waited upon by the landlord's three wives, miserable looking drudges, one of them apparently only fifteen or sixteen years of age. The Blue Beard of a husband had been there for eighteen years, and stoutly defended the institution. On our way to Uintah station we passed a picturesque band of Indians, men and women on horseback. Both sexes rode in the same manner, astride their ponies, and were dressed in gaudy colours, armed with revolvers, and their faces daubed with red paint. We obtained a good view of the Mormon valley while on the stage. This valley, with the lake, is surrounded by the Wahsach range of mountains, varying from 3000 to 4000 feet in height. Mountains, valley, and lake, alike present a fit locality for the perpetration of the Mormon deeds of darkness, and were doubtless selected by Brigham Young because of their gloomy isolation beyond the pale of civilization. There are a few lakes of fresh water amongst the mountains, fed by the everlasting snows, but for which no human being could exist in this desert wilderness of sand and wild sage. In these fresh water lakes are abundance of excellent trout.

After leaving Uintah, we passed through a great stretch of plain, lying between the Wahsach and the Humboldt mountain ranges. Almost as far as the eye could reach, nothing but sand was to be seen, not a hill or a tree in sight; even the water had to be brought a long distance on trucks, so wretched, dry, and arid is the country. Chinese labour has constructed nearly the whole of the Central Pacific Railway, and most substantially is it done. The Chinese are excellent labourers, steady, and industrious, more easily paid and more easily managed than the Irish out on these plains. We passed a good many Indians at some of the stations, along with their squaws and children. The babies are carried in a little basket or frame of wicker-work, to which they are strapped, and slung over the mother's back, the face being protected by a hood, also of wicker-work,—a "tight little arrangement," as one of our smart lady passengers—a girl of fourteen or fifteen, travelling alone!—called it. The Indians gaped with wonder at the train and the passengers, as we hissed along through their hitherto unfrequented wilds. At the stations the passengers presented them with peaches, grapes, and bits of ice, with which they appeared to be well pleased. One little fellow had already learned enough of English to ask for "pudding." The resemblance of the Chinese labourers on the line to the Indians was very marked, when the one was seen standing beside the other; the high cheek-bones and black hair of both were almost identical; the chief difference being in the colour, which may be accounted for by the difference of climate and style of living, the Chinese subsisting chiefly on rice, the Indians on the produce of the hunt. That both have sprung from one stock we cannot doubt, so that the present immigration of Chinese may only be history, after the lapse of ages, again, under different auspices, repeating itself.

Sierra Nevada Mountains.

But we are nearing California at last, and are climbing with our iron horse the sides of the Sierra Nevada Mountains. The railway passes over the summit at a height of 7000 feet above the level of the sea. The road winds and zigzags round and over the mountains in a most extraordinary fashion. Sometimes the train will pass along the edge of a precipice from 1500 to 2000 feet in depth, as for instance at the "Blue Canyon." These mountains and valleys are covered for hundreds of miles with a magnificent forest of pine trees of enormous dimensions, some of them being from one hundred and fifty to two hundred feet in height, and about six to eight feet in diameter, straight as an arrow. The railroad passes through the forest, the timber felled in the way serving for sleepers, bridges, and snow-sheds. The bridges on the line appeared to our European notions to be unsafe structures, being often very high, and merely built of trees bolted rudely together. When a train passes over them, they shake, creak, and tremble, as if they were going to tumble down under the weight. We passed under a wooden tunnel forty miles in length, put up to keep the snow off the line in winter. The arrangements of the Central Pacific Railway, or western portion of the line to California, are excellent, both on the line, and in regard to the accommodation for passengers. The scenery also is much more interesting than that on the Union Pacific, or eastern portion of this great through line.

Passing Dutch Flat, Gold's Run, and other mining stations, nestling in the romantic nooks and glens of these everlasting hills, peopled by Scotch, English, Irish, Germans, Chinese, and almost every nationality under the sun, all pursuing one object—gold—we began to descend the Pacific slopes of the Sierra Nevada Mountains, and speedily reached Sacramento, a city of ten thousand inhabitants, the then terminus of the railroad. At Sacramento we embarked in the steamer "Yosemite" on the River Sacramento for San

G

Francisco, distant 135 miles. Extensive orchards lined the banks of the river for many miles, the trees laden with fruit—peaches, grapes, pears, &c. At San Francisco we found the table constantly laden at breakfast, luncheon, and dinner with abundance of beautiful fruit, including almost every variety usually cultivated under glass at home, and of similar fine quality. The price of fruit in California is surprisingly small, and sometimes the gardens are so overloaded with fruit, that passers-by are notified to walk in and eat free of charge. A considerable portion of the traffic upon the Pacific Railroad consists of the conveyance of this superabundance to the great cities of the Eastern States. The Garden of Eden could scarcely have been more prolific than these magnificent Californian lands, which produce squashes weighing 300 lbs. in weight; gooseberries (which will grow nowhere else in America) like onions for size; peaches from trees only eighteen months old, with fruit of every description in rich abundance, and of unsurpassed excellence of quality and flavour. Of strawberries, in the season, San Francisco alone consumes some twenty tons daily; forty to sixty bushels of wheat is produced per acre for twenty years in succession without any manure; and of barley 120 bushels per acre. Straw being a drug, the ears of the grain merely are reaped, and the straw set on fire. The climate is singularly favourable, and the temperature remarkably equable, only varying in the city of San Francisco from 60° in summer at mid-day in the shade to 40° in winter. Inland, however, beyond the immediate influence of the sea breeze, the temperature is much higher in summer. Altogether California is a charming country, and with its auriferous riches, in addition to its extraordinary agricultural productiveness, it must become eventually one of the grandest states of the Union. The periodical occurrence of earthquakes is almost the only objection to it as a place of residence; in every other respect it is a delightful country—a land of

Goshen, full of plenty, where the soil is surpassingly rich, yielding luxuriant crops with merely a scratch, and without a tithe of the labour and expense bestowed upon our comparatively barren land. What would not our Scotch farmers give for such a country and such a climate?

The water of the Sacramento River is red in colour and muddy, arising from its clayey banks, and is full of excellent salmon, the only fish with which we met that reminded us of home.

On landing at the quay at San Francisco we were assailed by a drove of hyenas in the shape of hotel touters, who yelled at the unfortunate passengers as they landed in a most demoniacal manner. "Lick House," "Occidental Hotel," "The Kuss," "Cosmopolitan," "Brooklyn Hotel," and I don't know how many more, were shouted, bawled, and "hollered" at us by a perfect Babel of voices. We were followed and jostled, and our baggage seized by dozens of these pestilential fellows like harpies from the "vasty deep." Escaping their clutches, we got into a street car, and reached our hotel at a cost of threepence each instead of a dollar, as it would have cost, had we succumbed to the importunity of our tormentors. Travelling and living in America has since the war become very expensive, and the traveller requires to be ever on the alert against the thousand and one dodges adopted by the smart Yankees, who waylay his pocket on every hand, and boast when successful in their raid upon the stranger. We located at the "Occidental" during our stay in San Francisco, and were very well pleased with the accommodation, this being one of the best hotels we found in the States.

CHAPTER XIX.

San Francisco.

"IN front of San Francisco are seven hundred millions of hungry Asiatics, who have spices to exchange for meat and grain." The words are Governor Gilpin's, who used them when discussing the future overland trade. The San Franciscans wish the city to be the main station on the overland route round the world. This handsome city is beautifully situated for trade and for picturesque scenery. It stands on a rising ground of small hills, composed of sand thrown up by the Pacific Ocean. The private houses are mostly of wood, it being considered safer than stone, on account of the earthquakes; but most of the public buildings are of stone, while many of the stores or shops are of brick, with beautiful fronts of cast-iron,—expensive, but substantial and elegant. One of the sights of San Francisco is the "Seal Rock," about a quarter of a mile from the shore, on which are hundreds of seals, preserved there as natural curiosities. They barked somewhat like a pack of dogs as they sunned themselves lazily on the rock. When returning from the rock we passed the San Francisco water-works, a lake twelve miles long, giving abundance of fine fresh water to the city. We passed also the "Mission Dolores," a village now deserted, but formerly a Spanish Roman Catholic Mission to the Mexicans.

The city of San Francisco contains a population of about 160,000, of whom 10,000 may be reckoned as Chinese, who are seen here in great numbers strutting about in their native costume, pigtail and clogs, all complete. The Chinese portion of the town composes a complete settlement of its own. We took a walk through China Town, as it is called, and found ourselves in China at once. We saw a few of the women; but, if it were possible, they were uglier than the men, and they apparently left all the work, both indoor and out, to their lords. The men are employed as house servants, washermen, and laundrymen, and we found that they could do up our clothes as neatly as European washerwomen at home. The following are specimens of Chinese signboards which we saw in China Town:—" Dr. Wing Yeun, cures all diseases;" "Quong-Yee-Sing & Co., Manufacturers and Dealers in Segars, Wholesale and Retail;" "Tay Wo & Co., Chinese Intelligence Office;" "Chin Ling, Washing and Ironing;" "Hab Sing," "Sam Kee," "Sion Lee," "Hung-Wo-Tong;" dozens of other Chinese signs there were, some in English, some in Chinese, and some in both. We had an interesting opportunity of seeing the working of Chinese labour at the Mission woollen mills, two miles from San Francisco, where five hundred Chinamen are employed in spinning, weaving, &c. With the exception of a few English mechanics, the operations are carried on entirely by Chinese labour, and the manager informed us that he could not wish for steadier or better hands. The Chinese are reputed to be great thieves, but this gentleman informed us that in five years' experience he had not had one case of dishonesty. The Chinaman is an apt pupil, and soon picks up a new trade, his powers of imitation being keen. He takes few holidays; but when he does take one, or when he falls sick, he always sends a man in his place, so that the work is never interrupted. Even if he should go home to China with the bones of a relative, he will adopt this plan, and by-and-by he will return again to his accustomed post. A strange custom this of returning the bones of the dead to the Celestial Empire, to mingle there with the dust of their forefathers. Ship-loads of dead Chinamen are actually amongst the exports of San Francisco! The Chinese acquire no property in America; they horde and send home their savings. They return themselves when they have enough, and even their dead they will not leave behind. They wear Chinese manufactures, eat Chinese food, and maintain Chinese customs; hence the disfavour with which most Americans regard them. They are looked upon as leeches sucking the blood of the country; birds of passage not entitled to the rights of citizenship. This Chinese question will grow and have to be faced, and may be the next great problem for American politicians to solve. Already some 60,000 or 70,000 Chinese are in California, and still they come; and despite the hatred of the Irish, whom they undersell in the labour market, they are working their way to the Eastern States as well as down South, where they will also come into competition with the blacks in the cotton fields. There are great differences of opinion regarding this Chinese labour question; but those who are for shutting out the Chinese from the States of the Union because they will not settle on the soil, and identify themselves with the American people, appear to forget that labour is the great want in America, in order to the development of the vast and almost inexhaustible resources of that glorious country. True, it would be better if the labourer would spend his wages where he earns them, and so increase the capital, which, equally with labour, is so much needed in a new country; but surely the poor Chinaman is entitled in free America to his liberty in this respect, and so long as he gives an honest day's labour for an honest day's pay, he is entitled to spend his earnings how and where he pleases.

Before leaving San Francisco we hunted up an old Dundee celebrity, ex-Bailie M., and took him by surprise. His wife and himself were not a little astonished to receive a morning call from old acquaintances from such a distance.

Having spent a few most agreeable days in the Golden City, we turned our faces homeward by the same route that we came. It was dark when we had sailed down the bay; but on the return voyage it was light, and we had an opportunity of enjoying the magnificent bay, one of the finest harbours in the world,—one hundred miles in length, and from thirty to forty in width. The country surrounding the bay is very lovely and inviting. We saw it in the dry season, when for five months not a drop of rain falls, consequently not in its best dress, the ground being parched and brown. A few days' rain works a magical change ; when clad in living green the scene must be one of surpassing beauty.

We reached Sacramento, and took our places in the cars at six o'clock. Profiting by our experience of the refreshment rooms on our westward journey, we had provided ourselves, through the kindness of a friend, with a capacious and well-stocked luncheon-basket, the extreme dimensions of which having attracted the attention of the conductor, we were compelled to unload the contents, and leave the basket behind, the carriages being here of less roomy dimensions than is usual in America. One of our party, with characteristic thrift, made the most of the situation by disposing of the empty basket to a Chinaman, who is as ready to trade as even a Scotchman, for a dollar. We could not but remark the tidiness of a large party of these Asiatic labourers who were to be our fellow-passengers for a time. Each had his bed and bedding neatly done up into two bundles, and slung at either end of the inevitable pole, used by the Chinese for carrying their burdens across their shoulders. Quiet, respectful, and orderly in their behaviour, and neat and clean in their persons, the conduct of these idolaters formed a contrast to that which would have been exhibited under similar circumstances by an equal number of so-called "Christian" English, Irish, or Scotch labourers, who would by their rude conduct have merited the term "Barbarian" when compared with the superior behaviour of John Chinaman.

On reaching once more the snow-sheds on the Sierra Nevadas we found that two days previously two miles of them had been burned down, the fire having been kindled, it was supposed, by the Irish, in revenge for the Railway Company having employed Chinese labour when the Irish struck work upon the line. This delayed us a few hours; but at length the road having been cleared, we proceeded. On the two previous days the passengers had been obliged to walk, their baggage being carried by the inevitable and most useful Chinese. Many of the great pine trees set on fire by the burning shed were still blazing, and the fire thus begun might continue till the rainy season came.

At Truckee, a small station on the line, we passed a number of Indian men and women squatting on the ground amongst the dust playing at cards. The men were dressed in cast-off European garments. The women also were dressed in a similar manner. Their thick, straight, black hair was cut short across the brow, and a gap left free for their faces, a fashion of hair-cutting which we had seen much nearer home, viz., in the Orkney and Shetland Islands. After leaving Truckee we saw a number more of Indian men, and women with babies; the babies, as before observed, strapped on the women's backs, and having a cover of basket-work over their faces to protect them from the sun. The babies are whiter and better looking than their parents. Doubtless, had we been able to talk "Truckee," and had been so disposed, we might have bought, for a trifle, one for a curiosity! The line of railway keeps the track of the Truckee River for about 120 miles. This river ends in a beautiful lake, which abounds in very large trout. The Indians spear the trout when going up the river, and fish for them when going down. As we proceed farther on our way towards the prairies fruit gets more expensive. Grapes now cost one shilling a pound, three large apples a shilling, pears—large, uscious, and delightfully refreshing—the same, and peaches eight for a shilling. At Echo Station we saw again numbers of Chinese labourers engaged on the line. Their dwellings were small cotton tents, in front of which some of them had erected boughs of trees to keep off the sun. These men live almost exclusively on rice and tea, and appeared wonderfully merry and comfortable in their little fragile dwellings out on these lone wilds.

On the prairie we passed numerous large herds of mules and cattle in charge of their owners—ranchmen, who feed their herds on the ranches or green spots by the margins of the rivers, their markets being amongst the miners in the Rocky Mountains. Despite the hardships of such a lonely life, and dangers from the Indians, who sometimes attack the ranchmen and carry off their cattle, Yankee energy and adventure never fail to appear wherever a dollar is to be earned.

On our return trip we had booked to St. Louis, which is a journey occupying uninterruptedly five days and five nights from San Francisco. This time we resolved to avoid the horrors of Salt Lake City and Omaha, and did not break our journey the whole way, an arrangement which we found much preferable to encountering the doubtful hospitalities of these cities.

We had thus again an opportunity of studying the habits and customs of the Yankees as exhibited in their travelling arrangements. Were thirty or forty ladies and gentlemen deliberately to undress and go to bed together in one apartment, in ordinary circumstances it would be thought a highly scandalous proceeding. But such is really and truly the way they do things on board an American " palace sleeping car," and though somewhat startling when first contemplated, yet it is wonderful how quickly one unaccustomed to such things falls into the way of doing as the Romans do. A most commendable characteristic of American gentlemen is their devotion to, and consideration for the ladies. In every possible way the ladies receive precedence, attention, and politeness. The rudest miner or ranchman is a gentleman in presence of a lady. This feeling of gallantry smooths much that otherwise would be unpleasant in the promiscuous mixing of the sexes in an American sleeping car. The couches being made down and the curtains drawn, the gentlemen usually retire to the balcony at either end of the car to take their evening weed, while the ladies undress and get into bed; or otherwise they contrive in some way or another not to see that interesting proceeding. The ladies sometimes do not show equal consideration for the sensibilities of the rougher sex. Thus: one of our party whose sleeping berth was in awkward proximity to the common lavatory, was imprisoned in his berth one morning for upwards of an hour, while a young lady, with great deliberation, performed her morning toilette, including the careful application of a due allowance of cosmetics, which, by the way, the ladies appeared to use with charming openness and simplicity. Our friend getting rather impatient of the young lady's prolonged operations, a hint was conveyed to her to that effect, but the lady's reply was, "Oh, just let him get up, I'll turn my back:" and so he did. On another occasion, as a gentleman of our party was occupying the lavatory, a lady in charming *déshabillé, sans* morning wrapper or dressing-gown, appeared to claim her "turn," and did not hesitate to urge despatch upon our friend, who was in equally primitive costume. Even more curious examples of the free and easy manners prevailing here were sometimes seen; as in the case of a lady and gentleman, entire strangers to each other (the latter by the way a general in the United States army, and the former an actress), who occupied during the day contiguous seats in the car. At night when these seats were converted into sleeping berths, the lady slept in the under berth, and the general in the upper, one curtain enclosing both within its folds. "Good morning," said the general to the actress, as we passed their berths one morning, "You are just rising like a flower," and the lady emerged from her couch and shook her dress about her on the floor of the carriage. She had managed to dress in her berth before getting up, a feat of some difficulty. Such is life in the cars, and though in the description it seems *outré*, yet in practice it is wonderful with how little impropriety the thing is managed.

Our British railway directors would do well to take a leaf out of the Americans' book, and provide sleeping carriages for long night journeys. The present cramped carriages are bad enough at any time, but for long night journeys they are barbarous, with the constant calls to "Show tickets," "Show tickets,"—just when one has managed to get into a little nap. In America, the railway ticket system is entirely different, and very much better than at home. The railway tickets are in the form of coupons, and are undated, being *good till they are used*. Each guard or conductor has an allotted section of road, and when he comes into charge, he delivers to each passenger a time card containing a list of the stations on the road over which he travels; on which also is sometimes stated the elevation of the various points on the route above the level of the sea, and other particulars interesting to the traveller. These cards and the coupon for his section of the journey, the conductor collects before taking his leave, when he is succeeded by another, who repeats the same operation. Certainly the distances being so much greater, and the number of passengers so much fewer upon the American lines, renders it less necessary to be continually checking tickets by night and by day as at home; but surely, in regard to night travelling at least, and especially for the longer journeys, a great improvement might be effected in our British system of travelling, which appears to have made exceedingly little progress during these twenty years.

The American railway cars, particularly Pulman's palace sleeping cars, Pulman's palace dining cars, and Pulman's palace drawing-room cars, are most elegant and commodious wheeled structures, containing many of the comforts and conveniences usually found in stationary residences. When we were there the Pulman Car Company were constructing a *church* upon wheels for the Californian Railroad; and since our return we have heard of a party of about one hundred who left Boston by special train for an excursion to San Francisco, a seven days' journey, without stopping, the train being entirely composed of these splendid Pulman carriages, in which meals were regularly cooked and served as in a first-rate hotel, with all the exhaustless variety for which Americans are famous; the bill of fare being printed daily by a staff of printers in the train, who also, with the aid of an editor, supplied a daily newspaper to the passengers, containing all the latest telegraphic intelligence from all parts of the world, obtained, by special arrangement, from the various telegraph offices which are studded along the whole of this immense line of railroad.

This railroad to California, we were informed, had proved a great success to the promoters, who had been largely subsidized by Government both in money and in land; each alternate square acre on either side of the line for ten miles having been given in free grant to the proprietors. There was therefore great competition betwixt the promoters of the Eastern and Western sections respectively, as to who should make the greatest length of road. To increase their miles, and thus increase their gains, appeared to be the object, not to get to California by the shortest route; at least only upon this principle could we account for the extraordinary "circumbendibuses" we frequently observed, where nothing could possibly have prevented the line from being made straight ahead. So keen had the race between the two companies become, that they could not apparently agree upon the point of junction, and so they shot past each other many miles in the making of the road before they finally agreed to form the junction at Promitory, where, so bad was still the feeling between them, that we had to change carriages in the middle of the night, in the howling wilderness,—no agreeable task. No other change of carriages took place till Omaha was reached, where there was being erected over the Missouri a handsome iron bridge, which, when completed, will obviate the change here also, and then there will be an unbroken connection from the extreme east to the extreme west of this great country—3000 miles.

Leaving Omaha, we proceeded on our journey to St. Louis by way of Nebraska, passing through a very rich prairie country, the luxuriant prairie grass waving from five to six feet high, a dense reedy mass, mingled with sun-flowers seven or eight feet in height. On the St. Joseph line (or "St. Joe" as he is irreverently called here), we got into a marsh, where the rails are about as level as a dog's hind leg, and there appeared some likelihood of the whole concern disappearing in the bog; however, we escaped being swallowed up, and safely arrived at Macon City. Large numbers of the Negro race began to appear now in this part of the country—men, women, and children. Rejoicing apparently in her newly acquired liberty, a dashing lady of colour, with a bright blue veil, joined us in our car, much to the horror and disgust of some of her white sisters, by whom she seated herself. "It is enough to serve us for our coffee," one of them remarked with a jeer, loud enough to be heard by the poor darkie in the blue veil. This, however, was an exceptional case, for in general we observed no insult offered to the blacks. Our conductor, with the politeness everywhere shown to ladies, before leaving us at Macon, brought in his successor to our car, and introduced him by name to a lady travelling alone, who would be thus handed over from one conductor to another till her destination was reached.

We again crossed the Missouri at St. Charles, cars and all, in a steamer. As we approached St. Louis the number of blacks increased. The country here is very rich, and the Indian corn taller and heavier than we had yet seen,—growing, in some instances, to the extraordinary height of ten or eleven feet. After a continuous journey per rail of five days and five nights, we reached St. Louis at six P.M. We were much amused by the paternal care which the police officers took of us, in warning us to beware the cabmen did not cheat us. We shrewdly suspected the rogues had another object in view, and that in fact they were in league with the 'busmen, for we found that the poor cabman carried us to our hotel for about one-half what we should have paid had we taken the advice of the "dark man dressed in blue."

CHAPTER XX.

St. Louis.

SINGULARLY enough, into whatever city of the States we entered, we generally found friends, and here in St. Louis we were gratified to find a relative whom we had not seen for thirty years, who showed us much attention and kindness, and contributed greatly to our enjoyment while in the city. We visited the spot where the slave-market was formerly held; "Shaw's Garden," and other points of interest. The latter is the property of a retired merchant, who generously throws open his handsome grounds to the public free of charge. The following quaint notification is posted at the gate:—

"Resolved, by a committee of ladies, that as the perfume of flowers is conducive to the beautification of their complexions, gentlemen be requested to refrain from smoking and spitting in the conservatories and greenhouses.

(Signed) REBECCA EDOM, Sec.

It is hoped the above will be respected.

(Signed) HENRY WALKER."

This Mr. Shaw is a bachelor, and, with peculiar taste, he has erected his tomb in the garden right in front of his own house. His house is also open for inspection two days in the week; likewise a Botanical Museum.

Leaving St. Louis by the St. Louis and Iron Mountain Railway for Pilot Knob, we proceeded to visit the far-famed iron district of Missouri. We reached the Knob, only eighty-six miles distant from St. Louis, after a most wearisome ride of five hours, through an uninteresting maple wood country, and during part of the journey by the banks of the Mississippi. We reached the top of the Knob, six hundred feet high, by the ascending mineral cars. This mountain is of solid ironstone, of untold value, the quantity being said to be sufficient to serve the whole world for a period of a thousand years. Notwithstanding all this wealth there were only a very few men working at the iron mine, or rather quarry, and only one smelting furnace, of small size, had been erected, producing only about ten tons of pig iron a day. Pilot Knob ironstone contains from fifty-five to sixty-five per cent. of iron; but there is another deposit near by, called Shepherd Mountain, which contains ninety per cent., and is highly magnetic.

The Pilot Knob and Shepherd Mountain ironstone extend for seven or eight miles; but it is supposed that ironstone extends here for a hundred miles square at least. So rich is the ore of the "Iron Mountain" in this district, that a horse-shoe has been forged out of the raw unsmelted ore. This district not only abounds in ironstone, but is also very prolific in lead, tin, copper, zinc, porphyry, granite, tiff, and lime. Tiff is a white heavy stone, and is used for making glass and adulterating white lead, and even flour! During the American war there was a battle fought down at Pilot Knob, in which General Price's army of twelve thousand men was defeated by a Northern force of twelve hundred. The battle took place at Fort Ewing, which is still visible in the valley. Here there are about twelve hundred bodies interred, unmarked by any cross or monument. We returned to St. Louis the same evening, and were seven hours on the way, being equal to a speed of only twelve miles an hour; and a very wearisome journey it was, for the cars were occupied by swearing, drunken miners, and, all classes being equal—no drawing-room cars here—we had just to submit to their company and their disgusting language.

On Sunday we attended worship in St. Louis first Presbyterian church, which is a handsome building, with an excellent choir of two ladies and two gentlemen, with organ accompaniment. The sermon was preached by the Reverend Mr. Wynne, on the Lord's Prayer, and was much above the average of sermons in our country. The day was very hot, so that we availed ourselves of the fans with which each pew was usually supplied. Even the minister freely plied his fan, not foregoing the luxury, or rather necessity, while engaged in prayer. Fancy one of our clergymen using a fan during prayer on a sultry August day in Scotland. Ah no, that would be too horrible an act of sacrilege; but it is quite orthodox to smother the poor man in a black gown, choke him with Geneva bands, and enclose him in a washing-tub-like pulpit! Thus are we fettered by that tyrant *custom* in good old Scotland.

In the evening we attended worship at a black Methodist church. There were about two hundred and fifty people present, all black, excepting our party, who were the only white faces in the crowd. The singing was conducted by a choir of black people in the gallery, similar to any other small Methodist congregation. The minister was a black man, assisted by two others of the same colour, one of whom gave out the hymns line by line, like the precentor in some of our Highland churches, and the other prayed. None of the congregation had books, for probably they could not read, and therefore the line was read out. The sermon was on the power of God, and the preacher went right through the Bible, from Genesis to Revelation, in a strange incoherent manner;* altogether it was one of the most curious productions we ever heard. At the prayers the congregation stood up and turned their backs to the preacher and faced the other way. After the sermon, a young black man stood up and requested all who felt so inclined to come forward to the

* For the gist of the sermon *verbatim*, see Appendix.

table and deposit their collection, while the choir would strike up a "right hearty hymn." First a young black woman stepped coyly forward to the desk and deposited her collection, and then many others, male and female, followed. Afterwards the "pan" was handed round to those who did not wish to make such a public exhibition of their offerings. It was a very interesting sight, and the audience was very attentive, and apparently sincere and devout. The last prayer especially was very impressive. Towards the end of it, the black preacher raised his voice and intoned in a plaintive, solemn, sing-song voice, very much the same as is done in the Church of England Cathedral service. Then the groaning and sighing and moaning got louder and louder, and the universal fanning more vigorous, the heat being excessive. The blacks, men and women, were all clean and nicely dressed, and altogether quite equal in behaviour and appearance to a similar audience of whites at home, and there was no smell discoverable in the church, any more than if it had been a white audience. The black preacher was dressed in ordinary everyday costume, black serge frock-coat, with a white tie. In America ministers never wear gowns, and in general the tie is black. There are also no pulpits, merely a platform, upon which the minister paces backwards and forwards. The blacks and whites have always separate churches; and rarely does a black appear in a white church; more rarely still does a white appear in a black church.

Having seen all that St. Louis contained of interest, we again betook ourselves eastward by the Ohio and Mississippi Railway to Louisville, distant 274 miles, fare twelve and a half dollars, drawing-room cars extra, as usual. This line is on the broad-gauge principle, and does not pay. The country we passed through was very good, but only partly cleared. The chief crops were Indian corn, and the trees principally birch. Most of the farmhouses and villas were of wood. It was dark and pouring of rain when we reached the River Ohio, which we had to cross before reaching the city of Louisville. It reminded us of our experiences at Omaha. We crossed on a ferry steamer, omnibuses and all. At this time the Ohio was very low, and the bank sloped down several hundred yards. The road was very rough, or rather there was no road at all, for it was merely the bank of the river over which we drove. As at St. Louis, they are also building here a large iron railway bridge with stone piers; and they are doing the same at St. Charles, so that, by-and-by, the ferry steamers will be done away with, and much need, for they are a great nuisance. The speed on this journey was about twenty-seven miles an hour. We reached Louisville at nine o'clock at night, having left St. Louis at seven in the morning. It is the usual thing to travel from morning till night, that being considered a fair day's journey.

We took up our residence at the Galt House Hotel, a new and splendid house, free from bugs and mosquitoes (a somewhat rare luxury in America), elegantly furnished, and excellently attended. Would that we had in our own country such spacious hotels in which to rest after a weary day! As usual in the Southern States, the waiters here were all blacks—liberated slaves—civil, kind, docile, but slow, slow, slow!

CHAPTER XXI.

Louisville and the Mammoth Caves.

LOUISVILLE is famous for its tobacco-curing establishments, and for its tobacco warehouses. The usual custom is to sell the tobacco every morning by auction, just as it comes in from the planters. A sample is taken out of the hogshead, and the sale is made according to the sample. All the porters and servants in the warehouse we visited were blacks. Some of them had been with their employers for twenty years, formerly as slaves, and know very little difference in their condition now that they are free. When any extra work is required they perform it cheerfully, but do not get any extra pay. The wage they are paid is twenty-five shillings a week all the year round, whether there is work for them or not. We were informed that, on the whole, the blacks here are working pretty well. One gentleman, a large employer of labour, told us that the South was much better without slaves; and this was the general opinion throughout that portion of the South which we visited. We visited a tobacco factory belonging to a Scotchman, and were shewn over it by his nephew from Edinburgh. Where will you not meet a Scotchman! This factory is a large building, having two or three storeys, with a lift to convey the tobacco up and down. It is here the tobacco is dried, sorted, cured, and then repacked and sent to Europe. The value of the leaf, as we saw it in the cask, was only about threepence per pound. When being cured, tobacco is very sensible of rain, and, we were told, makes a capital barometer.

While taking our ease at our inn here one evening, we heard an alarm of fire. The next minute we saw flying past the gleaming fire-engines, the fires already burning in their furnaces. Embracing the opportunity of seeing how they do these things in America, we sallied out and followed the cry. Reaching the spot, we found the burning property to be a drug store and a furniture warehouse. Already five steam fire-engines were at work, each with its complement of firemen, engineer, and stokers. The passage of the machines through the streets from the depôt to the scene of action had sufficed to light the fires and get up steam. The hose were fixed and the water playing on the burning building in an incredibly short space of time. Within six minutes of the first sounding of the alarm bell, the engines, bright and orderly, were upon the spot, and in full operation. In about one hour the flames were extinguished, and the fire-engines away home. At the corners of certain streets in the various quarters of each city there is a telegraph apparatus, from which an instant alarm of fire can be communicated to the depôt, where an attendant is constantly in waiting, who instantly rings a bell to announce to the firemen that their services are required. At the same moment he sets a light to the fires already prepared in the fire-engines, the passage through the streets suffices to get up steam, and thus the whole machinery is in operation before the fire has got the mastery. Were our insurance offices to organize such a system as this at home, one-half the losses by fire, and an equal proportion of the premiums paid for insurance, might be saved.

We left Louisville on the 8th of September for the worldrenowned Mammoth Caves of Kentucky. We were called at half-past five; but from delay by 'bus and at the railway station, it was nearly eight o'clock till we got fairly off, so slow is locomotion in America. The Yankees cannot boast of smartness in their travelling arrangements. In this case, instead of arriving at Glasgow Junction (the station for the Caves) at a quarter past eleven, as advertised, it was one o'clock before we reached there, though the distance was only ninety-one miles, being at the rate of only about sixteen miles an hour. The scenery along the line was very interesting—beautiful hills and valleys, similar to the scenery of Killiecrankie. On the way we passed some small fields of tobacco growing, the first that we had seen in the field. It resembles our common dock, and well deserves the name of weed. On reaching Glasgow Junction, instead of finding " Proctor's stage " waiting, as advertised, to carry us to the Cave, still seven miles distant, we found a wretched wooden inn, where an attempt was made to delay us, so as to compel us to stay two nights at the Cave Hotel instead of one; the stage and the Cave Hotel belonging to the same proprietor. Such are the smart dodges tried on by our cousins over the way to turn an " honest " penny !

This was the sort of talk we had with this smart Kentucky innkeeper at his wretched tumble-down shed at Glasgow Junction, where " Proctor's first stage is always waiting to convey passengers to the Caves:"—

Traveller. " Where is the stage to convey us to the cave ? "

Landlord. " It's coming."

Trav. " So is Christmas; but we want to get on now."

Land. " Well, dinner's ready."

Trav. " But we don't want any dinner."

Land. " Well, sit down, be quiet !"

Trav. " But we won't sit down; we have these tickets to the cave, and must be taken on at once."

Land. " Your train is late; had you come in time the stage was ready.

Trav. " Two blacks won't make a white. Where's the stage ?"

Land. " Take a rest then. Some of them want to have dinner."

Trav. " We don't want dinner and we won't wait. We have no time to spare, and must get away."

Land. " Oh yes! you'll get away."

Trav. " Yes, but when ?"

Landlord, whittling his stick, turns coolly away.

Traveller (following up). " We insist on getting off at once."

Land. " Well, you'll get off. Sit down and be quiet !"

At length, seeing we would neither buy a dinner we could not eat, nor wait till the rest of the passengers had vexed their teeth in the attempt, " a first-class stage " appeared, in the shape of a wretched tumble-down rope-wrapped spring van, into which a quantity of luggage and ourselves were consigned. The little " man " that drove us had been twice up at the Caves that same day, and was in a terrible temper at being sent again. No doubt, if the wretched horses could have spoken, they would have sympathized with him. This little Jehu, in a towering rage, with his stage, came tearing up to the platform. Pat, the Irish waiter, who, as usual, came from Scotland *too*, cries out to the boy, " Take them boxes with you." The said boxes lay on the opposite side of the road at some distance.

The boy screams out in a bursting passion, " Why did you not tell me that afore ?" and paid no attention to the boxes.

" Take them boxes," said Pat.

" Bring them then," says little Jehu.

" Take the stage round," says Pat.

" Can't turn it," says Jehu.

" Go for the boxes," says one of the gentlemen to whom they belonged.

" Come and put them in then," says Jehu.

On inquiring at our hot-tempered Jehu—a boy of fifteen—

if it would be he who would bring us back from the Caves. He said, "Don't know. It'll be me or another 'man.'" Boys are men, and as for girls they are all "Madams," and carry themselves accordingly in fast America. At St. Louis we heard of a precocious couple who had been married, the boy at sixteen and the girl at fourteen!

After a delightful drive through a maple forest, we arrived at the Cave Hotel at three in the afternoon, just in time to go through the Cave. The whole party numbered about fourteen, and were accompanied by a black guide. We were three hours underground, but in that time only did the "short route." The "long route" occupies twelve hours, and extends nine miles in and nine out. Our journey was four in and four out. At the entrance each visitor was provided by the guide with a small lamp or cruise, and then proceeded single file, the guide leading. The Cave is sixty feet wide and forty high. The ground is quite dry, with heaps of large stones piled on each side of the path. We passed disused saltpetre vats Nos. 1 and 2, which the rebels in 1812 used for making gunpowder. There are also a number of hollowed out trees which they used for conveying water from the mouth of the Cave. The waggon tracks and footmarks of the oxen which brought in their supplies were also shewn us. About a mile from the entrance we passed two miserable huts, where four consumptive patients had at one time lived, thinking that the air of the Cave would cure them. One died in the Cave, and the other a short time after leaving it; and it is no wonder they perished, for a more miserable place—shrouded in darkness that might be felt—as a place of residence could scarcely be imagined. In the Cave is the Giant's Coffin, a large block of stone, not unlike a coffin in shape; the Methodist Chapel, an apartment resembling a place of worship; the Giantess, a peculiar figure on the ceiling; the Star-Chamber, so called from the star-spangled appearance of the roof of the Cave at this point. The Gothic

Chapel, a mile from the entrance, is a large room, from the ceiling of which hang gigantic stalactites, extending to the floor, giving it the appearance of a cathedral. The Devil's Arm-Chair, in the "Gothic Avenue," is a large column, about five hundred yards beyond the chapel, having a niche or seat in it. The weary explorer of the Cave is fain to seat himself even in this ominous chair, to rest a while. The ceiling of the Gothic Avenue is singularly beautiful, the stalactites assuming the most fantastic shapes. The Bottomless Pit and the Bridge of Sighs are on the main route to Echo River, and a mile and a half from the entrance. The pit is of an immense depth, and over it is thrown a substantial wooden bridge, across which visitors pass in the long route and towards Pensacola Avenue. The pit presents a sight of awful sublimity when its steep sides are lighted up by the guide. The altar consists of four pillars, also of stalactite, where two couples have been married,—one last fall, and one some years ago. One of the ladies promised to her mother on her deathbed not to marry the man on earth, so she went below the earth to save her promise, and have her own way notwithstanding.

This cave is a most strange phenomenon. Rivers, lakes, and waterfalls are found in its dark recesses. In one of the rivers there is a small fish, somewhat resembling a silver-fish, only the head is rather flatter, and it is quite blind, having no use for eyes in its strange abode. There is also another small creature found, like a miniature lobster, also blind. One could wander nearly two hundred miles in the wonderful avenues and streets of this underground city; but if once he lost his way, there is not a chance of ever regaining, unassisted, the light of day. The temperature is usually about 59° and it is very equable, while the air is pure and sweet. The only living animals we saw in the cave were a rat and some spiders. The dried skeleton of an Indian was once found in one of the avenues. It was supposed he had gone to hide himself and had lost his way, and so died. The State of Kentucky is pierced with these wonderful underground recesses. There are other two within a short distance of the Mammoth Caves, called the Diamond Cave and Proctor's Cave.

Much gratified by our visit to these surprising regions, although not at all charmed by either Procter's stage or his miserable hotel, we departed next morning on our return to Louisville, the morning beautifully bright, and thermometer 56°. Having dined at our old quarters at Louisville, we took the cars for Pittsburg *viâ* Cincinnati. Passing through a finely wooded and rather hilly country, with valleys cultivated with corn and the tobacco plant, we arrived at Cincinnati, the " Queen City of the West," at nine P.M., having travelled at the rate of only twenty-two miles an hour. We crossed the Ohio in an omnibus by the splendid iron suspension bridge, the widest in the world, the span being one thousand feet from pier to pier. The footpath of the bridge, when the river is low, is one hundred feet above the level of the water. We left Cincinnati at ten P.M. for Pittsburg. A delay of four hours occurred from an accident on the line, by which four men were killed, and two engines and six waggons destroyed. We passed them on our way down, and it was a terrible sight. The waggons had caught fire, and some of the soft goods were still burning, although they had been cast into the river.

We were very much disgusted on this journey at breakfast by a man indulging in one of America's besetting sins— profane swearing. It was probably the same individual who swore in the adjoining stateroom the previous night, much to our annoyance in the car. One fast young gentleman found it so slow in the cars that he had to go on the engine, just to get along a little faster!

We arrived at Pittsburg at six in the evening, instead of twelve noon, the hour at which we ought to have arrived, and having secured rooms in the hotel, we crossed over the

River Monongahela, which here joins the Alleghany, and forms the Ohio. Pittsburg is built on both sides of the river, and is a smoky place, like Dudley or Wolverhampton. The town and surrounding district contain about 200,000 inhabitants. There are numbers of iron, glass, and other works here, but they are small in extent, similar to our third rate or fourth rate works at home. Their pig-iron smelting furnaces are small, being only about twelve feet in diameter. Their malleable iron works are also on an insignificant scale, compared with our British iron works. The iron-stone is brought from the State of Missouri, &c., but the coal, which is of excellent quality, is got hard by. Skilled iron workers earn from nine to twelve shillings a day, and labourers about four and sixpence, working nine hours a day. Ordinary pig-iron was selling at about £6 per ton, and charcoal pig-iron at about £22.

We left Pittsburg at half-past eight in the morning for Washington (*viâ* Baltimore), distant 333 miles, which we reached at ten o'clock at night. We did this journey on the Pennsylvania Central Railway, the first double track road we had met with in the States, and one of the most difficult of construction. The line winds over the Alleghany Mountains, turning and twisting in an extraordinary manner, so that sometimes a long train becomes doubled into the form of a horse shoe, as it clambers up the sides of the Alleghanies, propelled by three powerful engines. The grade was sometimes as much as 900 feet in twelve miles; notwithstanding which the unusual speed of twenty-eight miles an hour upon the average was kept up, and even thirty-two miles an hour was sometimes attained. The scenery on this journey is very grand, especially on the banks of the Susquehanna and Juminata Rivers, where we could see numbers of fresh water tortoises basking themselves in the sun.

CHAPTER XXII.

Washington: Churches, White and Black.

ON Sunday we went to morning service in the first Presbyterian Church, the Rev. Dr. Sutherland's, and had the honour of being shown into General Grant's pew, which was merely one of the ordinary seats in the body of the church, with nothing to distinguish it as the President's. We knew it was so, from his name being upon the Bibles we used. In the afternoon we attended a very interesting prayer-meeting in this church in connection with the union of the two bodies of Presbyterians in America. After the service Dr. Sutherland, with that free and easy attention to strangers for which Americans are distinguished, came and shook hands with us, and spoke a few words of kindly welcome. Getting into conversation with him, we asked what had been the cause of the division in the Presbyterian Churches, which had now been so happily re-united. His reply was characteristic of the shrewd, plain, common sense of America:—" Oh," he said, " they had a big quarrel forty years ago, but now they see that the one party is just as good as the other, and so they have shaken hands, and are to say nothing more about it."

When will our Scottish Presbyterians take a leaf out of America's book, and cease their endless discussions about union, which are enough to nauseate all concerned? Why don't they shake hands, and be done with the subject? If Christian people were more entirely actuated by the true spirit of Christ, surely they would be less disposed to quibble and split hairs on all hands. Why, ah why, should there be so much of the Pharisaical " Stand off, I am holier than thou," amongst us. Surely a Presbyterian, free or bond, or only a U.P., may sit down with Abraham, Isaac, and Jacob; even although the Anabaptist, Independent, or it may be Episcopalian, sit down at the same table—(why not even a stray Roman Catholic)? And if they can do so above, why not below? "Behold how these Christians love one another," was once said; but may not the world now point the finger of scorn, and say, "See how they quarrel and fight!" Let the good people of the various Christian denominations in these islands imbibe somewhat of the freedom of glorious America, and, casting to the winds the big quarrels of forty or four hundred years ago, shake hands, and see that, after all, the one party, if they hold fast the grand first principles of Christianity, is just about as good as the other.

On the evening of our Sunday in Washington we attended a black church, of which there are some six or eight in the city. The church was crowded, the heat considerable, and the fans universal. The passages even were crammed by eager listeners. A numerous staff of well-dressed young blacks attended at the door to find seats for the audience as they arrived. It was interesting to see their attention, especially to the fair darkies, who came in crowds, dressed in the gayest attire—blue, white, red—in silk, gauze, and muslin, with fans and parasols in the latest style. Near us sat several elegantly dressed young ladies; one in particular almost a pure white, handsome, and even beautiful, but having in her veins the black taint, she could not attend church with the white folks even in Washington, the capital of the liberating North! Our party were of course the only whites present. The services were very lengthened. Preliminary to the preaching there were many prayers by different members of the audience, in that singularly simple but plaintive and touching style peculiar to black people. There were also many singings, conducted after a very strange fashion. One of the young men who had been so active at the doors would read out a verse—it might be of a chapter, a psalm, or a hymn—and then he would lead off and sing it to a tune apparently improvised on the spot, the audience following him vigorously in all the mysterious turnings and windings, ups and downs, of the extraordinary tune. One of the verses sung in this way was—

> "He that believeth shall be saved: he that believeth not shall be damned."

This was sung, like the rest, to a nondescript tune, the last word being pronounced with a peculiar shudder and sigh.

Unlike the black man at St. Louis, the preacher on this occasion gave out a text, 1 Peter iv. 13. He got on pretty well for three quarters of an hour or so, but his style gradually changed as he proceeded, till by-and-by the audience began to get excited, and sighing and groaning prevailed generally over the audience. This appeared to add zest to his eloquence, for the more the sobbing and sighing the louder grew the preacher's denunciations, till fire and brimstone seemed to flash from the big excited black man's lips, as he flung his sprawling arms around him, and swung himself to and fro upon the platform. The swelling sighs and suppressed groans of the audience now grew louder and louder, and incipient screams seemed to rise from the poor excited creatures as yet more terrible words flew from the excited preacher.

We could endure the scene no longer, but rushed from the place, to the surprise, no doubt, of the poor darkies, who appeared entranced by the infernal eloquence of the dark Demosthenes. We could not but regret, as we left the scene, that these evidently impressible creatures had not a milder gospel preached to them.

CHAPTER XXIII.

Washington.

WASHINGTON, "the city of magnificent distances," may also be called the city of great expectations, but expectations as yet unrealized. The site is grand, the streets wide, the plan unexceptionable. Dotted over the expansive plain are the public buildings of the nation, for the most part conceived upon strictly economical principles, the vast intervals being filled up by exceedingly common-place private buildings, with many unoccupied sites still unbuilt upon, waiting for occupants which never come.

The Capitol, or Congress House, occupies a good site on rising ground, and is built of white marble. Its handsome dome, glistening in the sun, is the chief feature of the city. America is a great country, but it cannot pretend to great buildings. The Capitol is only a piece of patch-work, and bright and showy as it is, it does not come up to one's expectations of the Parliament House of such a great nation. The foundation stone of the present building was laid in 1851 by the then President Fillmore, and occupies an area of three and a half acres. The grand Rotunda contains eight pictures, representing scenes in American history: Discovery of the Mississippi by De Soto, May 1541; Baptism of Pocahontas, Jamestown, May 1613; Declaration of Independence, Philadelphia, July 4, 1776; Surrender of General Burgoyne, Saratoga, October 1777; Surrender of Lord Cornwallis, Yorktown, 1781; General Washington resigning his commission, Annapolis, December 1782; Embarkation of the Pilgrims, July 1620; Landing of Columbus, October 1492. Leaving the Rotunda by the southern door, we come to the Hall of Representatives. This chamber is one hundred and thirty-nine feet long, ninety-three feet wide, and thirty high, and has seats for two hundred and eighty members, besides galleries for the public, the reporters, and the foreign ministers. It is a handsome chamber, painted in white, yellow, and gold. It occupies one of the new wings, and is surrounded by committee-rooms, &c. The other wing is occupied by the Senate Chamber, a much smaller and plainer apartment, also surrounded with offices. The Library of Congress is a plainly fitted room, ninety-one feet long and thirty-four wide. The collection of books numbers 70,000.

We also visited, in rapid succession, the other national buildings. At the Treasury we witnessed the printing of greenbacks by primitive hand-presses in the attic, while in the cellar we saw women carefully pairing the old greenbacks with scissors, and assorting them afresh. Thus humbly does Brother Jonathan carry on his vast monetary business. The White House, the residence of the President, is a very plain, old-fashioned, square house, of no pretensions whatever, and was undergoing, when we were there, a white-wash, of which it stood very much in need. The Patent Office and Post Office are still humbler buildings than the Treasury, but yet sufficient apparently to accommodate the business of the nation. The Navy Yard at Washington is very similar to the navy yards of the other cities which we visited, presenting a beggarly account of empty boxes. When in America we anxiously inquired for the navy and the Monitors of which we had heard so much. At Norfolk we were told, " Wait till you get to Philadelphia; guess you will see some Monitors there." At Philadelphia we visited the Navy Yard, and saw a grass-grown wilderness, with two or three small ironclads much the worse for wear, and not such as we should like to go many hundred yards to sea in. But here again we were told, "Wait till you go to Washington; guess you will see something there of the American navy." Again we were disappointed. But "Guess when you go to New York you *will* see Monitors and ships of war," again we were told. At New York, however, we were informed that we need not spend our time going to look for the American navy, for, in truth, navy they had none worthy of the name. Both in regard to ships of war and merchantmen America is nowhere. Never was it truer than now that "Britannia rules the waves." Shipbuilding is a defunct art in America, and will continue to be so, as long as she continues, by her protectionist policy, to shut out the free importation of iron, the material for modern shipbuilding. Agriculture is the backbone of America, and she should leave manufactures to the over-peopled European nations—Britain, Germany, France, Belgium—where labour is cheap and skill abundant.

Before leaving Washington we visited Ford's Theatre, where the mad actor shot President Lincoln. The theatre is a mean place, and has not since been used. The house into which the President was carried to die was pointed out—a plain street tenement.

We could not help regretting that so much venality and corruption prevails in the governmental and municipal offices of America, and, worst of all, on the bench; but surely a great future is in store for a country which places at its head such men as honest Abe Lincoln and General Grant.

CHAPTER XXIV.

Richmond.

ON a bright and beautiful morning we embarked on board of the steamer at Washington, and sailed down the Potomac, the width of which varies from half a mile to four miles—Maryland on the one hand and Virginia on the other. Leaving Mount Vernon, the former residence, and now the burying-place, of Washington, on the right, and also Fort Washington, which forms a defence for the capital city, we reached Aquia Creek, famous as the base of supplies during the war. Here we took the cars for Richmond, and were particularly pleased with the easy lounging cane chairs with which the cars were supplied, the most comfortable and cool that we had met with.

Passing through Fredericksburg we could see from the carriage windows the effects of the battle which was fought in the end of 1862 between General Burnside and General Lee. Numbers of the houses which had been destroyed by the cannon balls had never been repaired, and were still lying in ruins; but, saddest of all, the burying-ground, where rest the remains of 15,000 men who perished in this battle. The burying-ground is on the face of the rising ground which the Southern army occupied, and is enclosed by a simple white-painted paling. The rows of graves had at the top of each a white-painted board, on which were the names of those interred; but sometimes the names were unknown, and five or six such bodies would be interred in one grave, merely labelled "Soldiers—Names unknown." The burying-ground, from a distance, looked just like a nursery plantation with its uniform ridges and white labels.

Richmond still bore marked traces of the horrors of war. Whole quarters of the city had been burned down, and had only been partially rebuilt. The blackened ruins of thousands of houses still remained to tell their sad tale. The people seemed impoverished and reduced, but there remained a spirit of determination to retrieve their fortunes. Major J. H. Claibourne, a cousin of General Lee, we found carrying on the business of an insurance agent. He told us they were for ever done with rebellion, and wanted to get back into the Union as soon as possible, and to efface as rapidly as they could the ruin of the war. Every one, high and low, was working heartily to restore their broken country. Much had already been done; soon the city would be rebuilt, and the marks of war obliterated. Nearly every second person you meet in Richmond is black; many more are blackish, and some are whitey-brown; others are white negroes, by no means beautiful, whose faces are pale, but whose lips are thick, their noses wide and flat. Their hair is flaxen in colour, but curly like wool—strange mixture of the characteristics of two distinct races in one individual. These men and women, of all shades, we saw pursuing their avocations diligently as waiters, porters, labourers, shopkeepers, masons, carpenters, and house-servants; in this latter capacity both men and women served. Our chambermaid was a man, and we saw male house-servants even washing out the floors. They are slow, but kindly, and appeared more willing and more efficient than the Irish of New York.

Major J. H. Claibourne, from whom we received much attention during our short stay in Richmond, accompanied us in a tour round the city, including the old tobacco warehouse which formed the famous Libby Prison. This gentleman, who himself was in the commissariat department, assured us that the Northern prisoners received precisely the same rations as the Southern army, but that these were latterly scanty enough. If their prisoners were starved, it was because there was a lack of food, not from any cruel intention. It was starvation, said another gentleman, that conquered us, not the North. Almost to a man the whole male population of Richmond had been in the army, and the isolated individuals who had not also given up their last dollar and their last bag of corn in the great struggle, were now ostracised from society. We visited one of the numerous tobacco manufactories in the city, that of Mr. Mayo, whose business was the production of chewing-tobacco, in the preparation of which we saw some fifty men, women, and boys engaged. The principal workman was a well-dressed, intelligent looking Negro, in a clean white shirt, who, Mr. Mayo informed us, had been with him as a slave upwards of thirty years, and still retained his old post as a paid servant. Many of the other workers had also been nearly all their lives in the same establishment as slaves. They were all well-dressed, clean, and tidy, and one knot of workers accompanied their occupation with a hymn, well sung in parts in a low dulcet tone, as they went on with the twisting and sorting of the weed.

Slavery, the cause of so much suffering, is an institution which we seldom heard defended, and nobody expressed a wish to have it restored. All appeared agreed that the South would get on much better without it. The South fought for victory rather than for slavery.

The prevailing notions in this country regarding the unhappy conditions of the slaves appear to have been much exaggerated. Individual cases of shocking ill-treatment there undoubtedly had been, and much that was wrong no doubt existed; but, as a rule, it appeared to us that the slaves were well treated and well cared for, and that they were probably as well, if not better off, than the agricultural labourers of Scotland. Even their religious training was by no means neglected, nor was the law prohibiting education obeyed. In the families of such men as Major Claibourne, the slaves were instructed by the young people in the rudiments of education, and joined the household in their religious duties. Those who inherited slaves fell heirs to a most troublesome patrimony, and probably the people of the South, very many of whom are conscientious Christians, were more to be pitied than blamed.

In Richmond there are African schools and colleges, which, however, were in vacation when we were there; but it is gratifying to know that provision has been made for the education of the blacks throughout the States, so that the problem of Negro capability will soon be solved, and solved, we believe, in the affirmative.

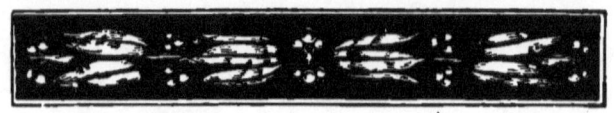

CHAPTER XXV.

Norfolk: Fortress Monroe: Philadelphia.

THE thermometer stood at 88° as we took our seats in the cars at mid-day by the Richmond and Petersburg Railway for Norfolk—distance one hundred miles. Our temper was not cooled by an encounter at the station with a rude member of the Southern "chivalry," who unceremoniously drove a perambulator over the toes of one of our party, and instead of an apology, merely remarked with the utmost *nonchalance,* "I did that myself," as if it was a piece of the finest breeding in the world to squash the toes of a Britisher.

We saw as we passed Petersburg, in the battered houses, sad memorials of the terrible struggle which here took place. Desertion and decay hung over the country like a pall, and it formed a melancholy contrast to the energy and life everywhere apparent in the Northern States. To add to the general desolation, we came upon a forest on fire, through which we travelled for about twenty-eight miles. On either hand for some five miles, nothing was visible but the crackling of the living trees, as they were being consumed by the fiery element. Had it been night, the scene would have been still more terrible. The fire had lasted for several weeks, nor was there any chance of extinguishing it till rain should come to drown it out. The loss of timber was enormous.

Having reached Norfolk—a thriving town of 30,000 inhabitants, we took up our quarters at a delightful little hotel, newly erected—the Atlantic. The Navy Yard at Norfolk, before the war, was considered one of the most important in the States, and was therefore eagerly seized by the South. Compelled at an early stage of the contest to evacuate Norfolk, the Confederates set fire to the Navy Yard. It is large and commodious, but deserted and grass-grown. The buildings and machinery are on a poor scale, and little work is being carried on.

Leaving Norfolk, we steamed down to Fortress Monroe, passing on our way the scene of the contest betwixt the Merrimac and the Monitor, where lay two small American ships of war. Fortress Monroe covers some sixty-five acres; walls well built and surrounded by a moat. In walking round the ramparts we passed the officers' quarters, where Jefferson Davis was confined.

Joining the steamer at Fortress Monroe we sailed up Chesapeake Bay to Baltimore. The accommodation on board was not of the best, and we could have wished that the Directors, and their insolent purser, had occupied one of their own hot and filthy berths in company with the myriad mosquitoes which that night feasted on their hapless passengers.

We reached Baltimore early in the morning, and had time before the train started for Philadelphia to take a hasty run through the city. Baltimore is a busy, bustling town, with some fine buildings and stores well stocked.

The Continental was our hotel at Philadelphia; charge the same as at most American hotels, viz., $4½ currency per day (the dollar being at the time worth 3s. 1¼d. sterling), everything included. The Quaker city contains upwards of three quarters of a million of inhabitants; the streets are comparatively narrow; the buildings of brick, and all of a painfully uniform design. Nearly all the streets are traversed by street railways, which are an indispensable convenience in

America, and one which doubtless will ere long become general in European cities also. Visiting a jute manufactory in the suburbs of the city, we were accosted by one of the workers from Dundee, who at once recognized one of our party. Her salute was—"Nae slaves here!" The condition of such workers is much better than at home, their wages being, for ordinary hands, $5 to $6 per week, while superior hands earn $7 per week; but this dear labour renders it difficult for the American manufacturer, even with the aid of a high protective duty, to compete with British goods. The proprietor of the above jute factory, formerly of Dundee, kindly acted as our guide to Philadelphia, and under his care we speedily visited the various points of interest. At the Navy Yard we were informed there were about " a thousand and a half " men employed. We were disappointed with its disorderly insignificant appearance, and with the poorness of the appliances. Little work was in progress, chiefly repairing ironclads. One of these, a turret monitor of the Merrimac class, had been in action at the bombardment of Charleston. Her sides, which were covered with four plies of iron plate one inch thick to the extent of four feet only, bore evidence of the work in which she had been engaged, the balls having smashed and indented her armour, but had not penetrated it. Her single turret was covered with plates to the thickness of eleven inches. A double-turretted monitor, which had accompanied Admiral Farragut upon his visit to Europe, was also examined by us, and we felt surprise that she had accomplished the voyage across the Atlantic in safety, for she possessed no bulwarks, but merely a flush deck, within four feet of the water's edge. Neither here nor at any other of the American Navy Yards did we see any ships of war for one moment to be compared with the ships of the British navy. The Mint at Philadelphia is a plain building of a useful and economical cast, into which anybody may freely enter to view and inspect the interesting processes connected with the coinage of the almighty dollar. The stamping of the coins is done by women with a very beautifully adjusted machine, which registers every coin it stamps, thus guaranteeing the honesty of the worker. Here there is a museum, containing a very complete and interesting collection of the coinage of every nation under the sun, including the " widow's mite " and Victoria's last florin.

From General Gregory we obtained an order to visit the Eastern State Prison, conducted upon the separate silent system, and containing accommodation for six hundred prisoners. On Sundays a clergyman preaches from the octagonal centre, from which the ranges of cells radiate, the cell doors being thrown ajar, so that the wretched inmates may hear the preacher though they cannot see him. Confinement alone without employment having been found so intolerable as to drive the convicts demented in some cases, a modification has been made in the originally strict rules in this respect. A cell is shown which had been beautifully painted by a prisoner long confined therein, who had thus relieved the horrors of solitary confinement. The whole of the walls were covered with a beautiful design in colours. Another cell, which had been occupied by a female prisoner, was similarly decorated with paper patchwork; and both exhibited no little taste on the part of the unfortunates who had been confined in these living coffins.

We admired the arrangement of the Public Library of Philadelphia, in which there was a most extensive collection of books; and the subscription, only $3 a year, included all the privileges of separate reading-rooms for ladies and gentlemen, newspaper-rooms, lecture-rooms, &c. The book shelves radiated from a centre, from which point the librarians could scan the whole. Instead of applying to the librarians for a book, each visitor helped himself, and reported to the party in charge, whose duties were thus very much lightened, and much time saved to the visitors.

Gerard College is the pride of Philadelphia. It was founded by one of her citizens, Stephen Gerard, who at his death left nearly £2,000,000 sterling for charities, of which this college is the chief, its object being the maintenance and education of orphan boys. The building is situated within handsome grounds, and is of the Corinthian order, erected in white marble. The founder sleeps in a marble sarcophagus in the entrance hall, surmounted by a marble effigy of himself, while in the attic of the grand edifice are still to be seen the humble chairs and tables which frugal Stephen used during his busy life, and the little curricle in which he rode. Would our millionaires not be happier and better men if they spent during their lifetimes a big slice of their useless wealth in works of charity and mercy, instead of building marble palaces over their own mortal remains, in which to train, doubtfully, a few children? Why do they not let the light and air of heaven in upon the wretched lanes and closes and cellars of our large towns at home, by sweeping away the filthy pent-up hovels that everywhere abound, and erect instead acres of model dwellings for the poor denizens of these lower regions? Missionaries and biblewomen know the hopelessness of the task of raising the masses till they are housed like human beings and not like brute beasts. Medical men know the impossibility of curing disease without air and light and cleanliness. It is a crying shame that, while we have many millionaires, and very many men of enormous wealth, we have so few Peabodys, and so few like Baroness Burdett Coutts.

When in Philadelphia we had an opportunity of hearing two remarkable sermons by the Reverend John Chambers, an "Independent Presbyterian." Reaching his church at ten A.M., the usual time of assembling in Philadelphia, and a much better hour than eleven, as customary in the old country, we found it to be a large and fashionable church, the platform handsomely "fixed" with marble pillars and marble screen, instead of a pulpit. The sermon was upon the religious education of the young, and was most eloquent and telling. Referring to the Sunday school in connection with his church, he freely mentioned the names of former scholars who now occupied high and honourable positions in the country. A thrilling effect was produced when he paused, and changing his tone, he pointed his finger to an empty pew, and said solemnly—" Last Sunday a widow sat in that pew with her only son by her side. Now the pew is empty, and the lonely widow weeps in her desolate home by the side of her dead boy." In the afternoon we returned again to hear the eloquent old man. His text on this occasion was the first chapter of Isaiah, and his object was to inquire " What, as a nation, they must do to obtain the favour of God." Applying the whole chapter, verse by verse, to America as a nation, he exposed in a scathing and impassioned manner their national sins and vices. He denounced his countrymen as Sabbath breakers, murderers, and thieves; the rulers as corrupt; the judges unjust; and mentioned that recently in Philadelphia it had been found impossible to get an honest man to collect the revenue from the spirit dealers, so that a tax-gatherer had to be procured from England, who, being found incorruptible, was basely shot. All honour to such sturdy faithful ministers as John Chambers of Philadelphia.

CHAPTER XXVI.

A Night on the Sound: Boston.

REACHING New York by the Amboy and Philadelphia Railway, and having dined at the famed Delmonico's, and paid three prices for that privilege, we embarked on board the steamer "Bristol" at five P.M., *en route* for Boston, *viâ* Fall River.

Projected by the notorious Jim Fisk and Jay Gauld of the Erie Railway swindle, the steamers on this line are floating palaces, got up with the utmost magnificence. The burden of the "Bristol" is 2962 tons register; engine cylinder 110 inches diameter, and 12 feet stroke; boilers 35 feet long, and 12 feet in diameter; speed 18 to 20 miles an hour. She has sleeping accommodation for 576 passengers, in 498 separate and spacious state-rooms, more like the bedrooms in a private residence than ordinary state-rooms on board ship. This floating hotel has four storeys. The lower storey contains a dining-hall capable of dining 110 at a time, where every delicacy of the season can be obtained at reasonable charges. The main deck contains the saloon or drawing-room, a splendid apartment, 300 feet long and 30 feet wide, richly and elegantly furnished, and carpeted with velvet pile in brilliant colours, and decorated in white and gold. The whole vessel is brightly lighted up with gas manufactured on board. Seven officers in uniform, gold lace and dress boots, receive the passengers as they arrive to embark, porters in white gloves being in waiting to open the carriage doors. Punctually to the time of starting the paddles went round, the splendid band of music struck up, and we were off with the speed of a railway train. Till the shades of evening drew in we enjoyed immensely the lovely scenery on either hand, and then one by one the hundreds of passengers retired to their respective chambers, to be lulled to sleep by the almost noiseless sweep of the vessel on the water, and the sweet low strains of the distant orchestra. All this luxury only cost three cents per mile. The fog horn awoke us as we approached Fall River, where we found railway carriages, some of them in the English style, by which we speedily arrived at Boston, the "Hub of all creation." Here we found comfortable quarters at the Riviere House Hotel.

Boston, a city of 300,000 inhabitants, presents more resemblance to an old country city than any other that we visited. Its streets are as narrow and irregular as Liverpool or Dundee, while its people are as aristocratic and conservative as those of Edinburgh or Bristol. Visiting the Exchange, at that time a mere cellar, we found a scene of extraordinary excitement, the New York gold rig being just then in full cry. As fast as the telegraph clerk could read off the announcements from the New York Exchange the price varied. We remained only a few minutes, but the price of gold advanced while we were there from 145 to 165! The same afternoon the price collapsed to 135. Such was the excitement that all business was entirely suspended, excepting business in gold. Many a fortune was lost, and many a career cut short on that eventful day. On the Sunday we attended service in the church formerly presided over by the elder Beecher, and for the first time in America had to stand at the door till the regular congregation were seated, a custom for which the minister, Reverend Mr. Martin, administered a rebuke to his people. Passing the Colosseum, a huge wooden erection, capable of containing 33,000 persons, where an Irish charity service was going on, we heard performing by the orchestra "The harp that once in Tara's halls," the audience joining, and producing in the distance a very grand effect. Being Sunday, however, it was saddening to think of such a performance going on on such a day. Such, however, we were informed, was a common occurrence amongst the Irish. In the evening we attended the theatre, where a Unitarian minister, Mr. Hepworth, delivered a farewell sermon to an audience of about 4000. The service was of the usual Unitarian character, painfully cold, chilling, and heartless, according to our ideas; the central light of Christianity being extinguished from their system. A large proportion of the Bostonians, we were informed, are Unitarians.

St. Lawrence is in the neighbourhood of Boston, and thither we were accompanied by a friend who had the *entrée* to one of the largest of the handsome cotton factories for which St. Lawrence is famed. Situated on the banks of a stream, the works are all driven by water power of great force and regular and ample supply. In the works of the Pacific Company, which we inspected, there were employed three to four thousand hands. The buildings were new, of substantial and excellent arrangement. On the premises cotton is manufactured through every stage, from the raw material to the finished cloth, including dying, printing, calendering, and packing for the market. The printing rollers are engraved on the premises, chiefly by women, aided by a most ingenious and intricate machine. As many as nine colours are printed simultaneously, and the whole establishment appeared to be very perfect and complete in all its arrangements. A library and news-rooms are attached for the use of the workers, one department for the men, and another for the women, erected at the cost of the proprietors. The working time is seventy-seven hours per week. Wages earned by girls attending four looms about $1¾, or 5s. 6d. sterling per day; mechanics $2½ a day; and young girls and boys 75 cents per day. The various companies have erected comfortable dwelling-houses for the work-people, who were well dressed; the girls with with bonnets and shawls, clean and tidy, and altogether apparently much more comfortable and of a superior class to the mill-workers of Dundee and other manufacturing towns at home. St. Lawrence is beautifully situated, and contains about 30,000 inhabitants, the whole of them connected with the various cotton factories,

Our friend also accompanied us to Waltham, where we had an opportunity of making a very interesting inspection of the American Watch Company's Factory. Here six hundred women, all well dressed and earning capital wages, are employed. In producing a watch, the different parts pass through one hundred and fifty separate operations, a special machine being employed for each process. These machines are of the most tiny description, and beautifully adjusted and adapted for the purpose to which they are devoted. We saw performed the delicate operations of coating the faces with porcelain, baking them in an oven, and lettering them with a camel's hair brush. One hundred and eighty complete watches are here produced daily, and are sold wholesale at about $25 each, exclusive of the case, which the company does not make. The wages earned by the female workers at this watch factory were about $1¼ a day currency (equal to 3s. 10d. sterling) on time, ranging up to $2 a day on piece-work.

After inspecting all the factory, we drove to the Cemetery of Mount Vernon, distant about four miles from Boston. The Cemetery is beautifully situated on undulating grounds, and beautifully laid out with walks and drives. The grounds were also well planted with trees, and there were also several fountains playing. In the centre of the Cemetery there was a beautiful granite chapel, containing four fine monuments of eminent Americans. The monuments are for the most part of white marble, but some are of American granite, and a few of red Peterhead granite all the way from Scotland. The designs were chaste and elegant, and the grounds altogether, in extent, arrangement, and situation very fine, and far superior in appearance to the celebrated Cemetery of Père la Chaise at Paris.

Driving through Cambridge on our return to Boston, we passed Washington's tree, and Emerson's quiet and unpretending residence, and called for a young friend at the students' quarters. We had an opportunity of seeing how economically and yet efficiently young America carries on his college studies. We spent a pleasant evening at Boston with friends whom members of our party had met in former travels in Europe. Here we also met a Scottish lady, a relative of Sir Walter Scott's, now, however, an American of the Americans, and an out-and-out Bostonian. The manners of society in Boston differ widely from those of the newer cities, and resemble more nearly those of the old country. Unitarianism prevails to a large extent, and high opinions are generally entertained of the perfectibility of human nature by means of education, training, and cultivation. Many of the ladies have a blue-stocking ring about them, which to our unsophisticated notions was less attractive than the simpler and less learned style of our own ladies of bonnie Scotland, who do not so often drive the bloom from their rosy cheeks by abstruse studies; confining their anxieties, with probably equal advantage, to humbler cares.

CHAPTER XXVII.

New York.

ON the 29th September, at 11·10 A.M., morning cool and clear, we left Boston for New York by the Lake Shore line of railroad; distance 231 miles; fare 2½ cents currency, about one penny sterling per mile; wonderfully cheap travelling, and good carriages.

The route lies along the shore of Long Island Sound, and is a pleasant ride through an interesting country, diversified by numerous inlets, in which villages and towns appeared prettily nestling. These inlets we crossed without changing cars, sometimes by means of piles, sometimes by boats, and sometimes by bridges. As elsewhere throughout the States, we found also on this line an iron bridge being erected to obviate the use of a ferry-boat. The important towns of Providence and New London lie upon this route, both formerly famous for their whale ships, before the "Alabama" ruined the American marine. Providence possessed an interest for us as being the residence of a remarkable old whaling captain whom we had met in our passage from Liverpool to New York. This man was a rabid teetotaller, a Baptist, and a zealous Christian. In season and out of season he energetically preached his beliefs, claiming respect and veneration even from those who differed from him most widely by his earnestness, knowledge, simplicity, and consistency. His weak point was tobacco. He could not deny he smoked five cigars a day all the year round, and his conscience was not altogether at rest on this point, as he was strong on the duty of consecrating the Divine gifts for the benefit of the ignorant and the conversion of the world. But as he devoted a fifth of all his earnings to Christian missions, he thought he might indulge in his favourite weed. If all were to follow the example of this plain Christian captain of Providence, how speedily would the world be Christianized! Where is the evidence of the sincerity of the Christianity of the possessors of fortunes which they can never use, yet whose contributions consist of the reluctant guinea, or, upon well advertised occasions, it may be a larger sum. But, ah, how seldom do we find any one giving away, like this honest captain, one-fifth of all his living! If such were the practice of all Christendom, how soon would be fulfilled the prayer " Thy kingdom come."

Reaching New York at 7·30 P.M., our train was conveyed well into the city along the public streets, engine attached, at the rate of about eight miles an hour, a contrast to the caution observed in the old country in permitting railway trains to pass through the streets even at a much slower pace. Upon reaching the more crowded thoroughfares, the engine was exchanged for horses, and proceeding upon the same track used by the street railway, we in this way were landed very near our hotel; on arriving at which, however, we found that one hundred and fifty visitors had that night already been turned away for want of room, and we were compelled reluctantly to accept of apartments on the sixth floor of the Hoffman House at the modest charge of six shillings each per night. Of the many modes of accumulating a fortune in New York, that of keeping a hotel in Broadway does not seem the worst.

Next day we visited Wall Street, the money market of

New York, where Jew, Gentile, and Yankee bankers most do congregate. Banks here are as numerous as whisky shops in the Saltmarket of Glasgow, or the Cowgate of Edinburgh. A friend introduced us to the shop in which he did his business, in the back room of which the banker sat with a pile of commercial bills before him, which he was disposing of to the highest bidder; his customers coming and going and examining the documents as they would a piece of calico or a bale of jute. The buying of bills he conducted upon the same plan, his customers bringing in the documents for sale as they would an ingot of gold, a bag of silver ore, or a casket of precious stones. Bills are thus discounted or sold without recourse upon any one but the party who has received the value represented by the bill. The drawer—that is the seller of the goods—is not held responsible to the banker, but only the party who grants the bill. The document is in effect a promise to pay the bearer. Every man has his price, and the discount charged for cashing the note depends entirely upon the stability of the promiser. Very weak names may require an endorser to make them go down at any price. By this free-trade mode of banking, a merchant is enabled at the close of every day's business to know where and how he stands, and what his profit or his loss. He sells his bills as he sells his cloth, and gets a price for them in accordance with the quality, which in this way becomes as well known in the market as that of any other commodity.

A commercial register is published in New York containing a list of the business houses in the principal cities of America, in which, besides other information, is recorded the probable price at which the paper of each can be negotiated. In selling goods, therefore, the merchant has only to refer to this register to learn the value of his customer, and he can adjust the price of his goods accordingly. Surely this is a more rational mode of doing business than that pursued in Scotland, where the charge for discounting all bills, whether of the first, second, or third class, is the same, but where the banker looks not only to the purchaser of the goods, but to the seller as well, for payment. The risk is thereby laid unduly upon the seller, who thus guarantees the stability of all his buyers, of whose position he has no certain means of judging, seeing that all paper is, by the Scottish mode of banking, fixed at the same value. By the American plan of free-trade in bill-discounting, the stability of every house is tried by the test of public opinion, and the price of its paper fixed accordingly. The banker is paid according to the risk undertaken, and the merchant is preserved from the excessive bad debts which are the blight of British commerce.

The excitement caused by the gold rig of the previous week had now subsided in Wall Street and neighbourhood; still, curses loud and deep were vented against the leaders of that famous enterprise. Gould, Martin, and Company, Jim Fisk, and others, were freely described as thieves, robbers, and swindlers; and a warm desire on all hands prevailed to lynch these gentlemen at the nearest lamp-post.

We visited the gold room, the scene of the madness a few days before, where, carried away by the frenzy of the hour, speculators wildly offered to buy millions of gold at 160, while others, only a few yards off in the same room, as wildly offered to sell millions at 140, but the Babel was so terrific that the one-half could not hear the other. The climax arrived when Secretary Boutwell threw two millions of gold upon the market, and broke the rig, while in maniacal despair one leading broker bared his breast and craved to be shot on the spot.

Separate from the gold room, which is a mean apartment, and more like a cockpit than an exchange, is the Stock Exchange, into which a friend introduced us. Here we witnessed the operations in Lake Shore Railway shares. The vice-president stood on the rostrum like an auctioneer, with hammer in hand, while the dealers were in front in a wild crowd inside of a railing, which separated all who were not members of the room. Each stock was taken in rotation, according to a list painted on the black board. The president decided when the business in any given stock was to be finished, and another stock brought on. Those who had stock to sell, as well as those who wanted to buy, then proceeded with a Babel of unearthly yells, which meant bidding; but of the purport of which none but the initiated could make head or tail. When the yelling and confusion outreached a certain point, and became so boisterous that even the preternatural ears of the vice-president could not tell what it meant, he smote violently on the rostrum with his hammer, till comparative calm was restored. As the sales were made the president reported them to a clerk at his elbow. When a stock was disposed of the last price was chalked against it on the black board; the next stock was then proceeded with, and so on till the whole was gone over. There are three exchanges or sessions of the board daily. The president has power to fine any one a dollar who bids the same price which has already been bid, or who bids after the hammer has been struck, indicating that that stock is past. In the intervals between the sessions of the board, and after the last meeting, the brokers deal privately in the long room, and when it closes adjourn to the street, where these keen worshippers of the almighty dollar still continue their operations. A telegraph company have connected the surrounding offices with the exchange, and for a moderate subscription annually, every office may be supplied simultaneously with quotations of every transaction done upon the exchange the moment it takes place. Look into any office in Wall Street and neighbourhood, and click, click, goes the machine, spinning out a paper ribbon, upon which is distinctly printed every sale as it is made.

One of the sights of New York is the retail store belonging

to A. J. Stewart, at the corner of Broadway and Eighth Street, a gigantic building of white marble, occupying a complete block. It is five or six storeys in height, the centre of the building being fitted up with galleries similar to the Crystal Palace, and lighted from the roof, which is of glass. The interior is elegantly fitted up and decorated, and the public are allowed to promenade freely throughout the vast premises, no one asking their business, or soliciting them to buy. When we were there, there could not have been less than from one thousand to fifteen hundred persons in the building, which is undoubtedly the most extensive drapery establishment extant. Electricity is made to do duty here as a lamplighter, the myriad gas jets throughout the establishment being simultaneously illuminated by a galvanic battery. A. J. Stewart has also an extensive wholesale store at the lower end of Broadway, where we purchased some specimens of American manufactures, and saw the old millionaire himself closely attending to his business, apparently as anxiously as when he came a penniless immigrant from Erin's Isle. Now he vies with Tweed, Vanderbilt, and Astor for the palm as the richest man in America.

We also visited the offices of the Erie Railway Company in Twenty-third Street, and saw the famous Jim Fisk and Jay Gould. Gould, said to be a bankrupt tanner, manages the affairs of this railway company, and informed us that the shares were as "good as gold." Jim Fisk, nine years ago, it is said, was a travelling pedlar, and is now, along with Gould, the owner of the great bulk of the Erie stock, of a dock at Jersey City, of the Opera House in New York, and is President of the Fall River line of splendid steamers. This Jim we saw in his shirt sleeves, very fat, and suffering from the heat. The offices, which are built of white marble, are most splendid in their construction. The floor of part was laid with polished marble, and the rooms are fitted up with beautifully polished and carved walnut, the different offices opening off a handsome vestibule, the divisions and doors being of walnut and plate glass. The grand Opera House is in the same block, and the entrances to it are fitted up in the same manner, only in a far more gorgeous style. The lamp pillars at the doors are bronze figures of exquisite workmanship. This splendid Opera House probably accounts for a portion of the dividends of the Erie shareholders. We doubt whether the investment may pay them!

The New Central Park is the Rotten Row of New York, where the wealth and luxury of the city may be seen displaying itself in all its pride and pomp. More worthy of a visit is the beautiful Greenwood Cemetery at Brooklyn, where the drives are said to extend to one hundred miles. Here we spent a very interesting day amongst the countless monuments and tombs, many of which were very handsome and costly. One of the most singular is a memorial erected by an old sea captain to his own memory. It consists of a full-sized statue of himself in marble, quadrant in hand, spying the sun. The old man used regularly to visit his own monument, till at last he was carried thither to return no more. The most elaborate burying-place is that of a young lady, who, at the age of seventeen, was killed by a fall from her carriage, and whose father, inconsolable for his loss, devoted her portion of his fortune to perpetuating her memory in marble. The Negro is allowed to sleep in Greenwood, but not amongst the whites—he has a corner to himself apart. This speaks volumes as to the black man's status in the North.

Brooklyn is estimated now to contain about 350,000 inhabitants, and there was being laid out for their recreation the New Prospect Park, which in extent and beauty will rival the famed Central Park of New York. The city is largely peopled by the merchants of New York, who have every facility of communication by the ferry-boats, which are large and comfortable, and the charge only a cent. They run every two or three minutes during the busy part of the day, and all belong to one company, which is restricted by Government to divide no more than ten per cent., the balance of their earnings to be spent on improving the ferries. But their profits being too large to be exhausted in the legitimate way, the proprietors have to adopt other means to make away with their gains, which is called in this country " cutting the devil round the stump," whatever that process may be. Brooklyn appears to be a very flourishing town, the shops and stores elegant and extensive. The City Hall and Courts of Justice are handsome buildings of granite. The Savings Bank is a prosperous concern, having about two million dollars of deposits, chiefly belonging to servant girls and the labouring classes. Alongside of the Savings Bank is a fire and thief-proof safe, for the preservation of the valuables and documents of the public. There is also a large Roman Catholic Cathedral, which has been in course of construction for the past two or three years, but owing to the massive nature of the work, it has only made a slight appearance above ground. When finished, it will have a splendid appearance, it being composed of granite.

On Sunday we crossed by the Fulton Ferry to Brooklyn, to hear Henry Ward Beecher. The day was pouring of rain, and very stormy, but we got the street cars direct to the church door. The church is a large, plain, square brick building, and not at all handsomely fitted up inside. It contains two thousand five hundred sittings, and has cane folding-seats for the passages, which makes it accommodate about three thousand. Strangers are allowed to occupy these folding-seats, and all the wall seats round the gallery. The strangers are also allowed to occupy all the seats not filled up by their owners within five minutes of the commencement of the service, which begins at half-past ten. The pews are let by auction, the cheapest pews, for four or five individuals, fetching about £11 a year, while as much as £300 a year has been paid for one of the best pews. Beecher himself, besides being a clergyman, is a fancy farmer on the banks of the Hudson, and we were informed that he returned his income last at $22,000 a year. Although the day was so wet and disagreeable, the church was about completely filled, the male community greatly preponderating, no doubt owing to the state of the weather. As usual in American churches, there was no pulpit, but merely an open platform, with a small table for the Bible. There was also a little pedestal alongside of this table, upon which was set a very handsome bouquet of flowers, and upon another little table by the side of the easy chair was set another similar bouquet. Behind the platform, at a higher elevation, is placed the organ, and in front of it sat the choir, consisting of two ladies and two gentlemen, paid professional singers, and fifteen other ladies and twenty-two gentlemen, unpaid. Dr. Beecher appeared entirely unattended, and with his dripping umbrella in his hand. He tripped lightly up to the platform, and put his hat, gloves, and umbrella down beside him; then he took off his topcoat, showing a bit of his shirt in the operation, and seating himself on the easy chair, he whipped up first one foot and then the other, and removed his indiarubber shoes. Taking up one of the notices, he scanned it for a minute, and then pitched it behind him; a second followed the first, but he retained the third. The choir then sang alone an anthem and chorus, accompanied by the organ, after which Dr. Beecher engaged very shortly in prayer. A hymn was given out from the "Plymouth" Hymn-Book, and joined in by the congregation. After reading, and another prayer, the sermon was commenced from the text, "Lay not up for yourselves treasures upon earth, where moth and rust doth corrupt, and where thieves break through and steal; but lay up for yourselves treasures in heaven, where neither moth nor rust doth corrupt, and where thieves do not break through nor steal."

Dr. Beecher appears to be in middle life, and inclined to be stout and ruddy, and has long flowing black hair. His dress consisted of a white vest, black tie, with collar folded over, black coat and trousers. Previous to commencing his sermon he read a notice for a collection in aid of a society for supporting western Negro colleges, and the collection was taken up in little baskets, which were handed round the seats, and finally deposited in two or three piles on the platform. After the collection was made, the sermon was proceeded with. Dr. Beecher's manner is peculiar, but not affected. He frequently sinks his voice into a conversational tone, and when he did so was not well heard in the gallery where we were seated. At other times he bursts into a flow of eloquent language. His great forte appears to be comic and pathetic alternately. Frequently a titter went round the church, and a nudging of neighbours at good points. Sometimes when he came to an important passage he would leave the table on which his manuscript lay, and walking backwards and forwards enact the part described. During the sermon, which lasted an hour in the delivery, Beecher made pointed allusions to the gold rig of the previous week. Two reporters sat just below the platform and wrote diligently, to one of whom, at the conclusion of the service, the Doctor handed down his manuscript.

But our stay in America was drawing to a close. Paying a few farewell visits, we once more took our passage in the "Cuba" for home, curiously obtaining exactly the same seats which we had occupied on our outward voyage, and accomplishing the trip home in precisely the same period of time almost to the minute, viz., eleven from days Liverpool to New York, and again from New York to Liverpool.

CHAPTER XXVIII.

Conclusion.

AMERICA is a country of such vast dimensions and such rapid growth that she has not yet got thoroughly licked into shape, and to any one accustomed to the staid and orderly state of things in Britain, she presents a youthful and somewhat chaotic appearance. If her age, size, population, and experience are considered, no wonder need exist that she is "a bundle of inconsistencies." Perhaps in nothing more than in her Indian affairs does she require amendment. In a new country like America, of such enormous dimensions, and progressing and changing with such rapidity, the Government has no easy task. The system also that prevails of changing the officials with every change of Government appears to be a thoroughly bad one. The result of the whole is, that the conduct of Indian affairs has been a complete failure under the Government of the United States, and acts of injustice and oppression of the grossest description have taken place, by which the poor Indians have been roused to acts of savage revenge. From Bishop Whipple of Minnesota, who has spent many laborious years amongst the Indians, we learned some of these acts of horrible cruelty and injustice, which are so gross and barbarous, that if derived from a less reliable source, they would be utterly incredible in a Christian land. The advancing tide of civilization has gradually driven farther and farther back these children of the prairie, robbing them of their fishing streams and their elk and buffalo runs, which forms the cause of never-ending disputes and fightings. The American Government adopted the plan of granting the Indians certain reservations of their ancient lands, restricting them within given boundaries; but in return for what they deprived them of, granting them by treaty certain equivalents in money, in agricultural implements, in seeds, in cattle, with missionaries to teach them and instruct them in civilization, so that they might till the land and settle upon it the same as the other subjects of the State. But these solemn treaties were broken and disregarded, and that not by the Indians but by the American Government and their agents. The promised pensions were left unpaid year after year, the promised seeds and cattle never came, the implements of husbandry never made their appearance, or if they did, the spades, instead of being steel, proved only shams of iron, and doubled up at the first trial; the axes were made of cast-iron, to sell and not to hew, and the seeds, if sent at all, were old and useless, and brought nothing forth. The poor Indian saw his wife and family starving, and dared not go out beyond his reservation to hunt or fish, and what could he do? The Indian agent, entrusted with the administration of the affair, was made rich by this atrocious knavery, and another agent may have arrived to repeat the same trick. The Indian feels that the great father at Washington has deceived him; he calls his braves together, and they go out upon the war path and put to death the first paleface they meet, burning up his settlement and destroying his family. The newspapers send forth a howl of extermination, and the soldiers of the Government are sent down to hunt to the death these poor, defrauded, exasperated savages. Such is the history of the great majority of what are called Indian wars—wars which are conducted by the Americans with atrocities which are enough to call down the vengeance of heaven upon the whole nation.

Black Kettle was a noble Indian chief, and always friendly to the American Government—in fact its slave. He at one time travelled two hundred miles to warn the mail-coach of an intended attack upon it by a hostile tribe. He had sheltered in his tent white men when in danger. His three brothers were also friendly; and in one of these wars they approached the American camp with flags of truce in their hands to mediate for peace. But to the everlasting disgrace of the American troops, all three were shot down in cold blood as they approached on their mission of mercy! This took place before Black Kettle's eyes. Seeing his brothers fall, he said to the white men whom he was even then sheltering, "You see what your soldiers have done to my brothers; but go to your camp in safety, it will never be said that Black Kettle proved untrue to any who had eaten with him." This noble Indian, the friend of the American Government, was afterwards blindly butchered in the same manner as his brothers.

On another occasion one of these wars had been concluded, and while a treaty of peace was being arranged, the officer in command of the American troops requested the Indians, four hundred in number, to come within their lines for safety, and they did so; but during the progress of the negotiations the American Government became of the opinion that the commanding officer was too favourable towards the Indians, and he was therefore superseded by a western general of exterminating proclivities. Upon taking his command, his first order was to butcher the whole of the helpless Indians, men, women, and children, who had come in good faith within their lines. The butchery took place with atrocities exceeding those of savage warfare, too horrible to describe, and not a redskin was left to tell the tale of blood!

Such are some of the contents of an official report on Indian affairs made to the American Government by order of Congress, by commissioners appointed for that purpose. So shocking and disgraceful were the facts brought to light in that report, that it was never allowed to be published. £5,000,000 sterling has been spent in these Indian wars, and thousands of lives of American soldiers have been sacrificed, almost wholly through gross mismanagement and jobbery. There are estimated to be still about 400,000 Indians of various tribes scattered throughout the North American Continent, some of them highly intelligent and noble men. Missions are in operation for their Christianization, and devoted Americans—some of them, such as Vincent Collyer, without fee or reward—are devoting their life's energies, under the auspices of the Government, to the welfare of the Indians.

Now that the Pacific Railway has rendered the country accessible, it will be much more under control; and it is to be hoped that, having got the South reorganized, the Government will be able to devote such attention to its Indian affairs as to prevent the repetition of similar horrors as those above referred to. Due allowance must be made for the enormous difficulties with which America has had to contend. We entertain a strong belief that she will speedily rectify the management of her Indian territories; wipe out Mormonism; drive her venal judges from the bench; purify her Government offices, and place honest men in her municipal chairs.

There is in America an electric energy on every hand. Bad men are very bad, and wickedness assumes its most daring forms. The river of life flows with a whirl and an excitement unknown even in this surging age in the old country. The race for riches in Chicago and New York is perhaps the fastest in the world, and the racers the most unscrupulous. The plunge for pleasure is perhaps the most desperate, and the draught the deepest. The young are sooner old, and the old sooner dead than in most other countries. The lamp of life burns with a preternatural intensity, and sooner goes out. But if the glare of the pit is fierce, the beams of the Sun of Righteousness are brighter still. The spirit of the Pilgrim Fathers lives in their children, and nowhere are there more devoted Christians than in America. The same resistless energy which pervades the workshops, the counting-house, the exchange, and the haunts of pleasure, extends to the pulpit, the Sunday school, and the missionary field. Who can doubt the result of the contest between evil and good? Who can doubt the glorious future of America, the boundless, the restless, the rich, the free?

APPENDIX.

SUBSTANCE OF A SERMON DELIVERED IN THE NEGRO CHURCH,
ST. LOUIS, MISSOURI,

SUNDAY, 5TH SEPTEMBER 1869.

WHEN I was thinking about what I would speak about dis evening, came into my head de power ob God. Dis den will be text:—" All power in heaven and in earth is in Thy hands; if it be possible, let dis cup pass from me, if I drink it." Who found dat diamond stone lying down dere, big as my fist? Who put it dere? God put it dere. De debil did not do it. But de debil did not help you find it. I suppose any man say you may have dis city, you might accept him. God said, " Partake ob all dat in de garden, but de day you eat ob dat tree you shall die." Now de debil transfers himself into an angel ob light, flies under dat tree. What power did he make use ob to fly under de laps ob dat tree? God's power! To show you all power belongs to God, take de three Hebrew children cast into de burning fiery furnace. Whose fire was dat? God's fire. Whose power was it when Daniel fell into de den ob lions? Was it not God's power enabled de king to throw Daniel into dat den? God's power! Whose power was it when de king said, " Fall down and worship de image?" It was God's power! How did de debil make war in heaven, and whose power was it he fought with? God's power! Whose power was it thrust him out ob heaven? God's power! Whose power was it put a chain round de neck ob de debil and throw him into de bottomless pit? God's power! Whose power brought you here dis night? God's power! If men had power ob dar own dey would resist de power ob death. He would tell death to go away dis time, and not come back again till dey sent for him. But all power in heaven and earth belongs to God. You see de lowest depth ob hell! He is dere! De king spoke when Jesus was handed up by de people. It was by God's power he spoke. Dat thief had more faith than Peter. After telling Him, "Though all men deny you, yet will not I never," he denied Him. It was done to show de power ob God. When He hung His head on de cross, den it was de power ob God. When He hung His head on His shoulder, de way was opened to heaven; de ladder came down from heaven. Again, I say, dat dat thief had more faith than Peter. When de rocks were rending, de dead saints rising, de dying thief cried out, "How reach me to heaven?" He had more faith dan Peter. Peter denied Him to save his poor miserable life. We find by de scriptures dat Judas betrayed; dat Peter denied Him; dat Thomas denied Him, but so soon as he had put his hand into de hole in de side, he said, "Dis is my Lord." So soon he had said dis, "Blessed is he dat believes, and has not seen." Blessed is de thief that believed this gospel. He that believes now may be saved—*shall* be saved; he that believes not shall be damned. The power is ob God, for de Apostolic saying is, "When I would do good, evil was present with me." All power is ob God. Again, we find dat Jesus, in using ob dis power, says—Solomon says—" The wisdom ob man is foolish." All power and wisdom is ob God. He lends it down to man, and he trades with it. I am going to believe dat when all men understands dis book—(the Bible)—dey have nothing to do but to close it and step down. If we can't get dar—(pointing upwards)—in dis way, we can't get dar till dere are so many dat you can't get in. So dey came to Jerusalem dey were sorry. Like de Quakers now-a-days, dey neber speak, except de spirit moves them. Dat will come back again. What power made dat man go and kill dat other man? It was God's power! We have no power. Dere is such a thing as a form of religion, and dere is such a thing as internal religion. Some people talk dat conversion is de same thing as regeneration; now it is as far different as de light ob de sun from de light ob de moon. A man goes wrong. I go to him and say, "You are wrong." He says, "Not I, I am too smart for dat;" but he finally agrees wid me, and comes back. He is converted—born ob God. He was born ob de Virgin! Now a man has got to be older dan de child. Now you say I am born again. Some ob you Christians have awful trials, I know dat; but I can't make peace between man and wife. What is peace? Old Job had a trial, and what power was it ? De power ob God. " De Lord gave, and de Lord takes away." Job was a true model ob a child ob God. Ebery time de debil came and bore de news to God, Job gave him nothing to carry back. Scrape dat old man; agitate him, and get him stirred up to swar. His wealth war gone; his houses war gone; his cattle war gone; his children war gone. " De Lord gave, and de Lord taketh away: blessed be de name ob de Lord." Though he destroy dis body ob mine; and I am proud to say that God has power to save dis body and dis soul. It was a body like mine, body and spirit, war gone preaching of His own gospel, and when done, when He stepped on de cloud de body and de soul war gone. De angel spoke,—" O men ob Galilee, why for stand looking up dar; He will come again." Coming not to consult with heaven or earth, Jew or Gentile. How will He come again ? He will reprove de world ob sin, ob death, ob righteousness, and ob judgment. Earthquakes, wars, storms, thunders! Look for His coming. All past. No saying when He may come. Can't tell when He *will* come. Be up and doing. Salvation in my right hand, damnation in my left—(sensation.) " Rise my love, my dove, my spouse, and come away!" We shall rise triumphant in dat day. *He* shall *rise*. De dead in de graves won't hear. Dey come here to-day. Dey won't hear to-day. We learn from de wicked men in de New Testament, " We'll hide in dat big cloud; but though you dwell in de lowest ob hell— (sensation)— my eye shall find him out." We shall sing 'deeming grace and dying love. Angels can't sing dat. All power in heaven and on earth is in my hands. De prophets, de disciples, for de blessing ob de world, had want of faith. What kind of army shall deir dry bones be ? Shall dey come togeder 'Zekiel ? How shall dese bones all be clothed ? Everything was in de right place. Shall every one ob dese bones live and breathe ? He breathes upon dem, and dey all stand up,—a great army. Eben though dis body sleeps in de grave a thousand years, he can breathe upon it, and it shall alive again. Nothing is too fine to war; but one man gives thanks and other don't. Now nothing is too fine to war, but lay down a nest egg for a rainy day. No sin in dat is thar ? What did he say ? He was not to touch ? Sin all over. If it was not for dese lights I could not tell de white from de blacks or de brown. Ebery one ob you can preach by your dealing wid one another. Don't gull dat man, though he is a little thin in de head. What you do to others He will turn back. We are de light ob de world. It would not stand war it not for us.

We are de light ob de world. All power is ob God! De world would not stand war it not for us. Get out ob de city, I am going to destroy it! Now we are de mainstay ob de world, and Christ prayed not to take out ob de world. I hab heard as many debils speakin' as any man. Man stay at home don't know much. All good you hear hold fast. I hab ever had dis same faith, and will hold it fast. Choose dis day, "As for me and my house, we will serve de Lord." "Go preach de gospel to ebery creature." "He that believes shall be saved, he that believes not shall be damned."—(Sensation.) Don't think coming here to church and paying dues will do. I am dis kind ob man, I take up de same ole cudgel. Dis book never moves. Men move away from it. If you go out and kill a man, don't think it is your power. It is God's power, and he will pay you for it. Dat young man who prayed to sink his soul to death—(sensation)—and he got it, as sure as you were born. Our land is pretty near being ruled by de debil. Sunday is race-day, gambling-day, drinking-day. Now hold up your colours. For all power in heaven and on earth is ob God. Amen.

www.ingramcontent.com/pod-product-compliance
Lightning Source LLC
Chambersburg PA
CBHW030317170426
43202CB00009B/1038